Peabody Journal of Education

Camilla Benbow, Dean, Peabody College
James Guthrie, Editor
Michele Thompson, Coordinating Editor
Matthew Springer, Associate Editor

Editorial Advisory Board

Darlyne Bailey, *Columbia University*
Sir Clive Booth, *Oxford Brookes College, England*
Mary M. Brabeck, *New York University*
Mark Bray, *The University of Hong Kong, Peoples Republic of China*
David W. Breneman, *University of Virginia*
Louis Castenell, Jr., *The University of Georgia*
David Chen, *Logistical Engineering University, Peoples Republic of China*
Lora Cohen-Vogel, *Florida State University*
Joseph P. Du Cette, *Temple University*
Donna B. Evans, *Ohio State University*
Victor Firsov, *Russian Academy of Teachers Retraining, Russia*
Juan Froemel, *LLECE/UNESCO-Santiago, Chile*
Mary Hatwood Futrell, *George Washington University*
Libia S. Gil, *New American Schools, Alexandria, Virginia*
Louis Gomez, *Northwestern University*
Gerardo M. Gonzalez, *Indiana University, Bloomington*
David W. Gordon, *Elk Grove Unified School District, Elk Grove, California*
Madeleine R. Grumet, *University of North Carolina, Chapel Hill*
Willis D. Hawley, *University of Maryland, College Park*
Phillip W. Jones, *The University of Sydney, Australia*
Martin J. Kaufman, *University of Oregon*
Kazuo Kuroda, *Waseda University, Japan*
Henry M. Levin, *Columbia University*
Denise Lievesley, *UNESCO Institute for Statistics, Canada*
Marlaine E. Lockheed, *The World Bank, Washington, DC*
James H. Lytle, *Trenton Public Schools, Trenton, New Jersey*
Ann Marcus, *New York University*
Bill McKinney, *Region IV Education Service Center, Houston, Texas*
Allan Odden, *University of Madison, Wisconsin*
Francois Orivel, *University of Bourgogne, France*
Thomas W. Payzant, *Boston Public Schools, Boston, Massachusetts*
Penelope L. Peterson, *Northwestern University*
Pam Saylor, *Lake County School District, Tavares, Florida*
Robert Slavin, *Johns Hopkins University*
Jandhylala B. G. Tilak, *National Institute of Education Planning and Administration, India*
Earl Watkins, *Jackson Public Schools, Jackson, Mississippi*
Steven R. Yussen, *University of Minnesota*

Peabody Journal of Education

Volume 80, Number 3, 2005

Rendering School Resources More Effective: Unconventional Responses to Long-Standing Issues

Introduction to the Special Issue on
Rendering School Resources More Effective:
Unconventional Responses to Long-Standing Issues   1
James W. Guthrie and Matthew G. Springer

An "Education Professions Performance Development
Act": A Prospectus for Providing "Highly Qualified"
and More Motivated Teachers and Leaders
for America's Schools   6
James W. Guthrie

Teacher Licensing in U.S. Public Schools:
The Case for Simplicity and Flexibility   15
Michael Podgursky

How Teaching Conditions Predict Teacher Turnover
in California Schools   44
Susanna Loeb, Linda Darling-Hammond, and John Luczak

Understanding the Relationship Between Student
Achievement and the Quality of Educational Facilities:
Evidence From Wyoming   71
Lawrence O. Picus, Scott F. Marion, Naomi Calvo, and William J. Glenn

(continued)

Assessing the Use of Econometric Analysis in Estimating
the Costs of Meeting State Education Accountability
Standards: Lessons From Texas 96
Jennifer Imazeki and Andrew Reschovsky

Exploring the Limits of Entitlement:
Williams v. State of California 126
Thomas Timar

Introduction to the Special Issue on Rendering School Resources More Effective: Unconventional Responses to Long-Standing Issues

James W. Guthrie and Matthew G. Springer
Department of Leadership, Policy, and Organizations
Peabody College of Vanderbilt University

America's K–12 schools now require more than $3 billion per day to operate, a figure that has been increasing faster than general price inflation for more than 50 years. The education systems quest for elevated outcomes, higher academic standards, enhanced instruction, practical performance incentives, and greater cost effectiveness has moved education finance from the periphery of policymaker concern to a far more central role. As a result, education financing is now a principal instrument for mediating educational policy.

Of course, education finance is a great deal more complicated than a half century ago and depends on superior understanding of education research, practice, and policy. For example, the field has transitioned from focusing solely on resource inputs to requiring understanding of complex relations between educational inputs, processes, and outputs. This transition has necessitated enhanced knowledge of production, market dynamics, and systemic alignment to better comprehend and improve education system realities.

Nevertheless, revenues to sustain schooling are large, and to date, schools have been virtually immune to productivity gains characterizing other sectors of the United States and world economies. If ways to render schools more effective can be determined, while not adding even higher school spending levels to the nation's fiscal woes, a double victory of elevated learning and decreased resource dependency may be possible.

Given the reemergent significance of education finance, Vanderbilt University's Peabody Center for Education Policy organized this issue of the *Peabody Journal of Education* (*PJE*) around the twin goals of schooling effectiveness and resource efficiency. The research and policy recommendations contained in this issue explore various facets of effectiveness and efficiency goals. Articles that follow address long-standing issues related to teachers, facilities, measurement of educational adequacy, and intersection of education policy processes and the legal system. Most if not all, however, do not necessarily arrive at conventional conclusions.

The first three articles in the issue directly address teacher-related matters. Approximately two thirds of U.S. school district budgets support teachers' salaries and fringe benefits. Hence, if schools are to be rendered more effective and cost increases stabilized, then considerable attention must be directed to teachers and teaching.

James W. Guthrie, editor of the *PJE* and professor of public policy and education at Peabody College of Vanderbilt University, addresses whether there is a fair way to escape the Procrustean bond of the single salary schedule that remunerates teachers for behaviors only remotely related to student achievement and inappropriately separates educators from labor market dynamics. He suggests that modern value-added measurement methods may offer an opportunity to accurately appraise teacher performance based on student academic achievement. Cognizant that scores of stages remain between what is presently known and what eventually must be known to enable this strategy to operate effectively, Guthrie proposes in his article a means by which the United States can nevertheless move forward on this promising front.

Michael Podgursky, the Middlebush professor of economics and chairman of the economics department at the University of Missouri–Columbia, appraises whether addressing the U.S. teacher quality problem by means of "raising the bar" in teacher licensing is likely to make matters better or worse. After reviewing extant literature and research findings, he arrives at a counterconventional conclusion suggesting that

> because there is so little reliable research to guide setting criteria for market entry, and such modest effects of teacher credentials in the current research, all such approaches are likely to accomplish is a reduction in the size of the teacher applicant pool with little change in the average productivity of the applicants. (p. 40)

Given such, Podgursky revisits economic roots and puts forth that "welfare is more likely to be improved if state regulators focus on what they can measure (student achievement), not what they cannot (teacher quality)" (p. 16).

Stanford University's Susanna Loeb, Linda Darling-Hammond, and John Luczak assess whether means can be determined for inducing a district's most able teachers to consistently instruct the most challenging students. By linking a relevant set of California databases, they examine how teaching conditions predict teacher turnover in California schools. The issue unearthed is at once more complicated than conventionally understood but also amenable to reasonable solution. Although teachers have long been assumed to dislike an assignment to hard-to-teach students, Loeb, Darling-Hammond, and Luczak find that "working conditions add substantial predictive power to models of turnover and that, when these working conditions are added, the influence of student demographics on reported turnover and hiring problems is reduced" (p. 64). They advise that reducing teacher attrition in hard-to-staff schools may necessitate salary and working condition improvements to surmount between school differences in teacher hiring and retention previously associated with student characteristics.

Operation and maintenance of school facilities accounts for approximately $60 billion, or 13% of total expenditures, in public elementary and secondary schools per academic year. Although as an accounting category it does not command anywhere near what is allocated for teacher salaries and fringe benefits, Jonathon Kozol's (1991) book, *Savage Inequalities*, and Bill Moyer's (1993) companion documentary, *Children in America's Schools*, brought school facility quality into the education limelight by painting a disparate portrait of America's school buildings across race and socioeconomic lines.

The fourth article in this issue, by Lawrence O. Picus, Scott F. Marion, Naomi Calvo, and William J. Glenn, takes creative advantage of one state's comprehensive facilities data to examine whether a systematic relation between facilities and student achievement exist. Proving one of the rare objective analyses, the researchers' analyses indicate that there is, for all intents and purposes, no relation between building condition or suitability (as measured by MGT building assessment scores) and student achievement (as measured by Wyoming's Comprehensive Assessment System scores). As a result, Picus et al. conclude that

> When resources are spent on facilities, generally there is less available for other programs that research shows can improve student learning. The substantial literature on the importance of high-quality teachers,

strong educational leaders, a rich and comprehensive curriculum, and parental involvement suggests there are other ways to invest educational resources that will have a greater potential impact on student learning. (p. 89)

Two decades of state-promulgated achievement standards and high-stakes testing, reinforced by the No Child Left Behind Act adequate yearly progress expectations and sanctions, have intensified a policy system quest to determine how much money is enough. Moreover, children's advocates and professional educator organizations have constructed an artful equal protection argument that relies on state learning standards as a means to propel questions of financial adequacy before courts as a constitutional issue. Therefore, officials in all three branches of federal and state government are persistently faced with the question, How much money is needed for an education system to be deemed adequate? Regardless of several emergent strategies to determine how much is adequate, answering the question has proven more elusive than might immediately occur to a layperson.

The fifth article in this issue is authored by two pioneers in the study of methods used for costing out adequacy, Jennifer Imazeki from San Diego State University and Andrew Reschovsky from the University of Wisconsin–Madison. Imazeki and Reschovsky artfully explain the significance of assumptions and modeling techniques in light of results of two econometric studies that arrived at differing dollar conclusions despite relying on similar data. Their article undoubtedly contributes to the existing knowledge base and further propels the utility of the econometric approach in determining how much is adequate.

Court decisions have had a remarkable effect on U.S. school spending. Indeed, 45 states have had constitutionality of their public school funding mechanisms challenged since the landmark *Serrano v. Priest* decision in 1971. Of these 45 states, more than 2 of every 5 have had a court render their respective funding mechanism unconstitutional. The final article in this issue of the *PJE* informs of an important issue of policy and process that resides at the confluence of education finance reform and litigation.

Thomas Timar, an associate professor of education at the University of California, Davis, examines issues of entitlement allied to *Williams v. State of California*—a court case challenged with determining "whether the state has a system of oversight and assures students adequate resources to benefit from the education provided them" (p. 129). Timar poses questions regarding the long-run utility of the significant success plaintiffs have enjoyed in recent adequacy suits and concomitant expansion of entitlements for students for the well being of the overall polity. He points out that among the most noteworthy changes in the system of education governance over the past 40 years is legalization, defining education issues as legal issues to be resolved by lawyers and judges. Nevertheless, Timar questions whether sole reliance on law-driven educational reform will truly improve schools.

References

Kozol, J. (1991). *Savage inequalities: Children in America's schools.* New York: Crown.

Moyers, B. (1993). *Children in America's schools* [Documentary]. Alexandria, VA: PBS Home Video.

No Child Left Behind Act of 2001, Pub. L. No. 107–110, 155 Stat. 1425 (2002).

Serrano v. Priest, 557 P. 2d. 929, 949–959 (Cal. 1971).

An "Education Professions Performance Development Act": A Prospectus for Providing "Highly Qualified" and More Motivated Teachers and Leaders for America's Schools

James W. Guthrie
Department of Leadership, Policy, and Organizations
Peabody College of Vanderbilt University

Classroom teachers are among the few remaining employee groups whose evaluations and remuneration are generally unrelated to their performance. However, it is difficult to appraise a teacher's effectiveness by achievement of pupils because learning is not under an instructor's complete influence. New measurement techniques are emerging, however, that offer a prospect of discerning how much an individual teacher's instructional efforts contribute to learning. This article identifies impediments to implementing "value-added" testing, recommends a development effort to address unresolved issues, and specifies components of a proposed Education Professions Performance Development Act that could direct federal resources. These recommendations include alterations to No Child Left Behind Act regulations to further a fair and accurate teacher assessment and reward system based on performance.

Requests for reprints should be sent to James W. Guthrie, Department of Leadership, Policy, and Organizations, Peabody College of Vanderbilt University, 230 Appleton Place, Peabody #514, Nashville, TN 37203–5721. E-mail: jwgxiii@bellsouth.net

This proposed federal legislation is intended to complement and facilitate purposes of the No Child Left Behind Act.

A sufficient amount is now known to be able to identify challenges to moving teaching toward a performance orientation. However, there exists inadequate knowledge about how to do it effectively, and we lack guidance in other cases about how to weave the knowledge we do have regarding performance pay into practical policies that districts can adopt and evaluate. Given such, there exists a necessity for a focused federal research and development (R&D) program and federal performance development act to accompany the No Child Left Behind Act.

Background

America's K–12 schooling is being strongly urged to adopt "standards and accountability" strategies symbolized dramatically in the No Child Left Behind Act. Whereas the United States once appraised schools by resources consumed, school performance increasingly is judged by learning produced. This outcome orientation is influencing the perspective and actions of state, district, and school officials; policymakers; and parents.

However, there is at least one important education sector where the performance orientation is not penetrating deeply. This is in the education profession itself.

No Child Left Behind Act and many state accountability systems contain sanctions for sustained low-performing schools. However, there are few incentives or disincentives for classroom instructors to be judged by their performance in facilitating student academic achievement. Indeed, teaching is the largest single professional undertaking still devoid of significant performance rewards. Even government civil service workers increasingly come under modern performance appraisal schemes.

This situation continues although there is much at stake. The direct financial costs of paying America's public school teachers approaches $2 billion per school day. On top of these dollars are the benefits that might accrue to students and societies if teacher expenditures were allocated in a more effective manner.

The Four-Point Challenge

A thoughtful reader will rapidly acknowledge the absence of performance incentives as a major education policy deficiency but just as quickly flinch once recognizing the daunting impediments to change.

J. W. Guthrie

The performance challenge contains four major facets, any one of which by itself necessitates a major development effort to overcome: (a) fair measurement, (b) effective incentives, (c) appraisal of preservice teacher training, and (d) more accurate means for measuring school administrator performance.

Fair Measurement

Judging an individual teacher's effectiveness based on students' academic achievement is difficult because a student's learning is not under immediate control of an instructor.

There are few more powerful social science findings than those consistently documenting out-of-school influences on students' in-school performance. Innate aptitude, parental commitment, early childhood environments, household resources, community amenities, peer group expectations, and personal aspirations are among the legion of individual conditions over which schools and teachers have only modest influence.

Past efforts to meet the performance pay challenge include compromise schemes, such as attempted in Cincinnati, whereby teachers were to have been rewarded for elevating professional skills thought to promote greater student achievement. Also, there have been a few "merit pay" and teacher pay-for-performance trials. However, to date, these efforts have failed for lack of objective measures and inability to control for the aforementioned out-of-school influences on achievement.

"Merit school" plans have also been attempted, whereby all teachers in a school are rewarded, regardless of specific individuals' efforts, if the entire school elevates student performance. However, such schemes encourage "free riders," a condition inevitably breeding dissatisfaction.

Given this history, it is no wonder that 96% of America's public school teachers are paid for their seniority and education levels. This is the ubiquitous "single salary schedule" against which policymakers and critics rant but which steadfastly dominates teacher pay. Even if bearing only a remote relation to student performance and disconnecting teaching from other labor market realties, years of service, and college credits, the nub of teacher salary schedules persist because they are understandable, objective, and quantifiable.

However, the standards and accountability movement, coupled with advances in measurement, may be placing a solution closer at hand. It may be possible to measure the performance of an individual teacher by calculating the addition to a student's achievement over that existing prior to the teacher's efforts. This is the so-called value-added approach to appraising student performance between two points in time.

Value-added strategies, and accompanying statistical techniques for holding student's out-of-school characteristics constant, although discerning effects of an individual teacher, are in their infancy and in need of further R&D.

Effective Incentives

Even if measurement issues suddenly were solved, questions would remain regarding effective means for linking achievement measurement with incentives for teacher performance. Some policy mechanism is needed to bridge this gap. What can serve as an appropriate incentive system for classroom teachers?

If teaching really is a "calling," then perhaps little or nothing can be done. However, if teachers, as individuals in an occupation, respond to the range of internal and extrinsic conditions that appear to move workers in other occupations, then there may be an answer.

One path worthy of policy pursuit is financial performance incentives. Teaching is one of the few remaining employment activities in which pay is consciously separated from the principal purpose of the organization. Also, if financial incentives are effective in motivating teachers to concentrate even more intensely on academic achievement, then, assuming elevated achievement results justify performance pay costs, it is a relatively simple solution to the nation's challenge of rendering schools more at reasonable costs.

If performance pay proves disappointing, then the challenge of elevating U.S. school productivity becomes even more daunting.

Teacher Preservice Training

The absence of a performance orientation begins early, even before many aspiring teachers assume classroom duties. The rewarding of process, rather than outcome, starts in teacher training in America's network of (a) college-based teacher training institutions, (b) school-of-education accrediting agencies and education school associations, and (c) companion bureaus within states responsible for teacher licensure.

Most state certification frameworks and college-based teacher training programs require "student teaching," a truly live performance endeavor. However, appraisal of student teachers' performance is seldom rigorous or comprehensive. It usually results in a simple letter grade.

There are a few innovative exceptions, usually where large school districts have taken advantage of "alternative certification" clauses and have organized their own preservice teacher training programs. However, the dominant preservice training model, reinforced by the aforementioned iron triangle of special interests, continues to judge teaching candidate performance by inputs, college courses taken, academic units acquired, and possibly a standardized pencil-and-paper test.

The idea of objectively measuring a teacher licensure candidate's instructional skill or classroom management capacity is not widely accepted. This is a policy domain where the No Child Left Behind Act, despite its requirement of a "highly qualified" teacher for each of America's students, has failed to gain significant traction.

Prospective teachers should possess (a) fundamental knowledge and communication abilities; (b) genuine expertise in one or more subject matter areas; (c) reading and mathematics instructional skills; (d) the ability to tailor instruction to student needs; (e) classroom management know-how; (f) a capacity to relate to a wide spectrum of learner backgrounds, disabilities, and student skill levels; (g) technical ability to construct and interpret tests; and (h) a capacity to communicate effectively with parents and citizens.

It is performance capacities such as these that should be measured, not number of college courses taken, time spent formally registered, or amount of tuition paid.

Administrator Performance

The performance of school administrators, principals, and subordinates is frequently evaluated. Moreover, these judgments are increasingly linked to the collective academic performance of students in their schools.

Presently, administrator appraisals are not always fair. They rightly rest on components of a school's success, such as community perceptions and parental satisfaction. However, when it comes to pupil performance, a principal's rating is too often not value added but, rather, the raw level of student proficiency in the school. In the same way that a teacher does not have student achievement immediately under his or her control, principals and their assistants cannot be held fairly for student achievement without taking student social and economic circumstances into account. All the needed R&D efforts mentioned previously regarding value-added testing apply to practicing principals as well as teachers.

What about the preservice career of principals? If a case can be made for the performance measurement of preservice teaching candidates, should aspiring administrators not be equally included in a performance measurement mandate? Somewhat ironically, the answer is no.

Few individuals enter school administration without having first been a classroom teacher. A good case can be made that such instructional experience is useful for all principals. However, whatever principals have undertaken prior to consideration for appointment to administrative posts, they almost always have a track record that can be appraised to ascertain likely success in the multifaceted world of school administration.

What Can Be Done?

The convention of certifying and rewarding classroom teachers and teacher candidates for generally irrelevant conditions, seniority, and academic course credits is long standing and deeply defended by many of education's special interests. To move the present teacher preparation system more forcefully toward performance measurement, one has to ensure that there exists a valid product, or set of products, for performance measurement.

Many claim they can "tell a good teacher when they see one." However, gaining empirical evidence regarding good and bad teachers is more difficult than simply relying on a viewer's narrow experience or intuition. The matter is made more complicated by the possibility that a good teacher for Johnny may not necessarily be a good fit for Suzie.

Mounting a major R&D effort to gain a more comprehensive understanding and capacity to measure teacher candidate performance traits can be a fruitful avenue. This can be a conventional but carefully managed R&D program engaging think tanks, research-oriented universities, bold school districts, charter schools, state education departments, and private sector R&D firms in competitively bid commissioned research.

Parts of this puzzle are already addressed. For example, where subject matter is crucial (e.g., secondary school physics, history, or mathematics), examinations already exist and can be purchased "off the shelf." Also, research in the last decade on reading and mathematics now suggests what teachers should know and be able to instruct effectively in these fields. Special education also is making strong progress in being able to specify what classroom teachers need to know to assist high incidence but relatively low levels of handicap (e.g., mild reading disability or speech difficulties) in children. Finally, the National Board of Professional Teaching Standards has pioneered techniques for appraising a classroom teacher's capacity to organize subject matter, present it effectively to students, and test their levels of knowledge.

An R&D effort is needed initially to weave these already-existing individual pieces into a practical whole that local schools and districts can use to appraise performance potential of teaching candidates. Subsequently, "experimental research" will be needed to validate the link between these performance measures and effective teaching.

Suppliers, almost regardless of the quality of their teacher performance appraisal "products," will be reluctant to come to market unless they perceive there is wide demand. The federal government can gain policy leverage on this problem through mechanisms such as (a) R&D focused on teacher testing and performance appraisal; (b) funding local school districts, charter schools, or states (rather than schools of education) to undertake pilot teacher training and alternative certification projects and experiments; (c) redefining high-quality teachers (in performance terms) in the No Child Left Behind Act regulations; (d) providing R&D funding to schools of education willing to break the mold and measure teacher candidate performance; and (e) redeployment of federal government student financial aid.

Only the federal government is in a position to propel these solutions. It is not advantageous for an individual state to bear the brunt of development costs only to see resulting benefits thereafter distributed to free riders. A federal initiative is in order. Hence, the Education Professions Performance Development Act (EPPDA) is proposed.

EPPDA

Preamble: Purpose of the Act

The purpose of this act is to further development of performance-oriented measurement techniques and performance incentives applicable to teachers in training, classroom instructors, and school administrators.

It is understood that these purposes are to be pursued through federally contracted development efforts directed at improving the application of value-added testing techniques enabling accurate identification of individual teacher's contributions to the knowledge of students, experimentation with performance incentives for teachers and administrators, and construction of performance measures relevant to preservice certification of teacher candidates.

Title I: Enhancing Means for Measuring Unique Contributions of Individual Teachers to Student Achievement

This title authorizes federal government funding and procurement of multiple development projects aimed at honing value-added measurement of student performance.

Title II: Enhancing Scientific Experimentation With Performance Incentives for Teachers and Administrators

This title authorizes federal government funding and procurement of multiple experiments aimed at designing and appraising the consequences of a spectrum of performance rewards for classroom teachers and school administrators.

Title III: Enhancing Means for Measuring Preservice Teaching Capacity

This title authorizes federal government incentives for researchers to construct and experiment with the application of valid preservice teaching candidate capacity measurement procedures.

Title IV: Education Professions Performance Act State and School District Grants

This title facilitates school and district employment of able individuals from programs such as "Teach for America" and "Troops to Teachers." These are alternative training and certification efforts that funnel candidates into classrooms without crucially depending on conventional teacher training. However, the capacity to instruct these alternatively prepared candidates should not go unmeasured simply because of a program's uniqueness or prestige.

Title V: Redefining No Child Left Behind Regulations Regarding Highly Qualified Teachers

Presently, No Child Left Behind requires states to have definitions of "highly qualified teachers." However, No Child Left Behind guidelines leave great discretion in this regard. These regulations could be narrowed to induce states to begin to define highly qualified for beginning teachers as those who have been apprised by the kinds of comprehensive professional performance processes discussed in earlier sections.

Title VI: Encouraging Alternative Teacher Training Suppliers

Expanding suppliers of teacher training even further beyond conventional college programs can be encouraged through at least two avenues. One strategy is to provide federal government development grants to charter schools and local school districts enabling them to design Request for Proposals (RFPs) to contract with alternative suppliers of preservice teachers. RFPs would be oriented toward performance appraisal of teaching candidates.

An eventual second means is to redefine student financial aid eligibility for teacher training candidates so as to authorize only those attending institutions that can show evidence of performance appraisal of their graduation candidates. However, operational implementation of such an innovation should await further validation of performance appraisal mechanisms. To move too fast on this dimension might be to lock in less than fully validated measurement systems before necessary R&D effort takes place.

Title VII: Administrator Performance Measurement

This title is the analog of Title I, concentrating on development of value-added measurement for teachers. However, in this instance, the development objective is to adapt individual student value-added measurement techniques to be appropriate for an entire school. Success on this dimension can subsequently lead to a No Child Left Behind Act amendment regarding "adequate yearly progress" for an individual school.

Practical Matters of Money

The aforementioned legislative proposal is a logical policy companion for the No Child Left Behind Act. It is not an expensive companion. The appropriation of relatively limited funds, approximating tens of millions of dollars if targeted as suggested, could gain significant leverage on the measurement of teacher, teacher candidate, and administrator performance and thereby begin to enhance the supply of truly highly qualified teachers and leaders for America's schools.

Reference

No Child Left Behind Act of 2001, Pub. L. No. 107–110, 155 Stat. 1425 (2002).

Teacher Licensing in U.S. Public Schools: The Case for Simplicity and Flexibility

Michael Podgursky
Department of Economics
University of Missouri—Columbia

Discussions of teacher quality in U.S. public schools have tended to focus on teacher licensing. Reformers from diverse perspectives have proposed "raising the bar" for licensing by various means (e.g., harder licensing exams, more coursework, graduation from the National Council for Accreditation of Teacher Education teacher-training programs, elimination of emergency or provisional licensing). However, all of these proposals assume that teacher licensing plays an important role in determining teacher quality and performance. In this article I argue the contrary. Raising the bar for teacher licensing in ways that have been proposed is unlikely to have any significant short- or long-term effects on student achievement. Moreover, by shrinking the applicant pool for vacancies, these restrictive proposals may have the perverse effect of lowering average teacher quality, particularly for high-poverty or rural districts that already face thin applicant pools. A preferred approach is to swap regulation of inputs for accountability for outputs, that is, a more

An earlier version of this article was presented at the Teacher Preparation and Quality: New Directions in Policy and Research Conference, American Enterprise Institute, Washington, DC, October 18–20, 2003. I thank Youn Soel and Erin Allen for research assistance, Michael Wolkoff and conference participants for many thoughtful comments, and the Smith Richardson Foundation for financial support. The usual disclaimers apply.

Requests for reprints should be sent to Michael Podgursky, Department of Economics, University of Missouri—Columbia, 118 Professional Building, Columbia, MO 65211. E-mail: Podgurskym@missouri.edu

flexible licensing regime that relaxes entry barriers combined with greater accountability for student achievement gains. Such a proposal is based on a simple economic principle: Welfare is more likely to be improved if state regulators focus on what they can measure (student achievement), not what they cannot (teacher quality).

Introduction: Six Propositions About Teacher Labor Markets

Teacher licensing figures prominently in popular discussions of teacher quality. On the one hand, teachers unions, the American Association of Colleges of Teacher Education, and the National Commission on Teaching and America's Future (NCTAF) have pressed to make teaching more like medicine with national teacher testing standards, mandatory accreditation of teacher training institutions, "independent" state teacher licensing boards, and similar entry restrictions (Ballou & Podgursky, 2000; NCTAF, 1996, 1997). Critics from outside of the mainstream education community have also targeted the teacher licensing process and called for more rigorous exams and stronger academic training (Ravitch, 1998; Walsh, 2004). Teacher licensing also figures prominently in the teacher quality standards of the No Child Left Behind Act. Among other things, states are required to phase out emergency and other types of "substandard" teacher licensing. Finally, shortfalls of fully licensed teachers figure prominently in school finance "adequacy" litigation where plaintiffs make the case that school spending is inadequate based on the higher incidence of inappropriately licensed teachers in low-income, high-minority plaintiff school districts (e.g., Darling-Hammond, 2003). Such arguments clearly played a role in the recent New York State court decision overturning the state school finance system (*Campaign for Fiscal Equity v. New York State*).

A common theme in all of these examples is a belief that teacher licensing plays an important role in determining teacher quality and performance. In this article, I argue that "raising the bar" in teacher licensing, based on the criteria advocated by reformers, is unlikely to have any significant short- or long-term effects on student achievement. Teacher quality in schools has much more to do with personnel policies such as incentive pay, performance reviews, dismissals, and effective professional development. Moreover, because various proposals to raise the bar shrink the applicant pool for available vacancies, they may have the perverse effect of lowering average teacher quality, particularly for high-poverty or rural districts that already face thin applicant pools. A preferred approach is a more flexible licensing regime that would relax entry barriers and permit school districts greater discretion in hiring decisions in exchange for greater accountability for student performance. To lay the groundwork for this argument, I begin with several propositions concerning research on teachers and the economics of occupational licensing.

Research Linking Teacher Training or Licensing to Student Achievement Is Inconclusive and Provides Little Support for Aggressive Regulation of the Labor Market

If policymakers choose to raise the bar or more rigorously enforce teacher licensing, they should have solid evidence that the criteria used to exclude teacher candidates from the market has a demonstrable relation to student achievement. Otherwise, such policies will simply shrink the size of teacher applicant pools without raising the average quality. How strong is the research base for formulating policy concerning teacher training and licensing? Recent surveys of the scientific research base find it is very thin.

Such an assertion seems to fly in the face of claims by various education groups about the "knowledge base" for teaching and certainly seems contradicted by the hundreds of studies published annually in education research journals, many of which are devoted to teacher education.[1] However, there is widespread consensus in the social science research community that scientific evaluation of social policy programs (including education) requires (a) randomized experimental study design or (b) nonexperimental longitudinal data on participants.[2] Unfortunately, little research on teacher testing, training, or licensing meets either standard, and the research that does is tentative and inconclusive.

---

[1] For example, a 1996 report of the NCTAF, a self-appointed commission including the president of the National Council for Accreditation of Teacher Education and the National Board for Professional Teaching Standards, stated, "Although hundreds of studies have shown that fully prepared teachers are more effective than those who are unqualified, the practice of hiring untrained teachers continues" (p. 15). "Teachers who know how to do these things [pedagogy] make a substantial difference in what children learn. Furthermore, a large body of evidence shows that the preparation teachers receive influences their ability to teach in these ways" (p. 27).

[2] A third model, most frequently used by economists, is the "natural experiment" model (Heckman, LaLonde, & Smith, 1999). This has not been widely employed in the teacher literature. An exception is Jacob and Lefgren (2002), who use longitudinal student-level achievement data for Chicago public school students and exploit a quirk in the administrative regulation to create a "quasiexperiment" to examine the effect of teacher training on student achievement. However, even with natural experiments, longitudinal data are highly desirable.

Randomized experimental design is the "gold standard" for social policy research. With respect to teacher quality, this would involve estimating the effect of teachers with different credentials or training on student achievement through random assignment of students to classrooms of variously credentialed but otherwise comparable (e.g., experience) teachers within a school. I am aware of only one study of teacher training or credentials that meets this standard, although the Institute for Education Sciences of the U.S. Department of Education is actively promoting such studies (Mosteller & Boruch, 2002; U.S. Department of Education, n.d.), and more are under way.[3] Thanks to these efforts, 5 years from now it is likely that we will have experimental evidence on teacher licensing and training.

If randomization is not feasible, and often it is not, then one must rely on nonexperimental data to evaluate education policy. If we are to measure the contribution of a classroom teacher to student achievement, it is necessary to control for prior achievement of the student before he or she enters the classroom. Ideally, researchers would pretest the students in the fall and test them again in the spring. The difference in these scores, averaged over the classroom, would be a measure of a teacher's "value added." If students are not pretested in the fall, then it is also possible to use test scores the previous spring, or for more than 1 previous year (longitudinal achievement data). Large longitudinal data files have formed the basis for the most sophisticated current research on teachers and teacher effects on student achievement (Aaronson, Barrow, & Sander, 2003; Rivkin, Hanushek, & Kain, 1998; Sanders & Horn, 1994).

Studies that do not have a rigorous study design (i.e., with randomization or controls for prior student achievement) are likely to produce seriously biased estimates of the effect of teacher certification or other teacher characteristics on student achievement. The reason is that they do not adequately control for the socioeconomic status (SES) background of students in classrooms, and student SES is correlated with teacher credentials and strongly correlated with student achievement. In the language of econometrics, cross-section studies of the effect of teacher credentials on student achievement suffer from "omitted variable bias."[4]

---

[3]A recent study of Teach for America (TFA) conducted by Mathematica Policy Research (Decker, Mayer, & Glazerman, 2004) used random assignment methods. They found that students taught by TFA teachers had significantly larger achievement gains in math. Estimates of achievement gains in reading were also larger, but the difference between TFA and traditionally trained teachers was not statistically significant.

[4]A recent study by Hoxby (2001) highlighted the importance of these socioeconomic variables and their potential for producing bias in studies of teachers and student achievement. Hoxby analyzed the effect of family, neighborhood, and school input variables on student

For example, consider studies of the effect of teacher licensing on student achievement. Given the complexities of teacher licensing systems, virtually every school district in the United States has some teachers out of compliance; however, substandard certification tends to be relatively more common in schools with low SES students. Because SES has a very powerful effect on student achievement levels and gains, unless the researcher has very good controls for prior achievement and SES in a study of certification and student achievement, the resulting study is likely to yield an upward-biased estimate of the effect of certification.[5]

The number of studies of teacher certification that meet the minimum methodological standards outlined earlier is very small. A recent survey of the literature by Wayne and Youngs in the spring 2003 *Review of Education Research* found only two studies of teacher certification that were peer reviewed, used longitudinal student-level achievement data, and controlled for student SES. The results of these studies (both by Goldhaber & Brewer, 1997a, 1997b, and both using the National Longitudinal Educational Survey of 1988) had mixed results. They did find a small positive effect of math teacher certification on math achievement, but no statistically significant effect of science teacher certification on science achievement. Recent surveys of the literature by Hanushek and Rivkin (2004) focusing on "high-quality" studies that meet the standards described earlier find little evidence linking teacher credentials to student achievement. For example, of nine estimates of the effect of teacher test scores on student achievement, six found no statistically significant

achievement and educational attainment using two large nationally representative longitudinal studies of students (the National Educational Longitudinal Survey [NELS], NELS88, and the National Longitudinal Survey of Youth, which began in 1979). Hoxby compared the percentage of the variation in student achievement on various field tests (math, reading) explained by school, family, and community factors. For every test, the percentage of the variation explained by the family variables far exceeded the school input variables. The family variables explained from 34 to 105 times as much variation in student achievement test scores as the school input variables. She also examined years of schooling completed at age 33. Family variables explained 19 times as much variation in student educational attainment as did school inputs.

[5]Moreover, this is not a problem that is "fixed" by meta-analyzing large numbers of flawed cross-section studies because all of these studies are biased in the same direction. Meta-analyzing 200 such studies simply produces a more accurate estimate of a biased coefficient. A target shooting analogy can illustrate this point. If the scope on a rifle is off or out of adjustment (biased), then the rifle shots will cluster around a point that is away from the target bull's-eye. Firing more shots will simply do a better job of identifying the point around which the sight is targeted but will not help determine where the bull's-eye is. That requires that the bias or error in the rifle scope be fixed.

effect. Of the three finding a significant effect, two were positive and one was negative.[6]

In short, the research foundation for raising the bar with teacher tests or raising standards for schools of education is weak. The evidence linking any type of teacher training, licensing, or testing to student achievement is mixed at best. Even estimated effects of general academic skills of teachers such as SAT scores, although usually statistically significant, are generally modest in effect.

Teacher Effects on Student Achievement Are Quantitatively Important but Idiosyncratic

Does this mean teachers do not matter? On the contrary, although the effect of measured teacher characteristics is small, one consistent finding is that there seems to be considerable variation in teacher effectiveness between classrooms. Therefore, if one compares the effect on student learning of the top and bottom 20% of teachers ranked by performance, the effect is often quite substantial. However, these teacher effects are largely unrelated to traditional measures of teacher quality such as licensing exam test scores, certification credentials, experience, or graduate degrees, a result highlighted in a recent survey by Goldhaber (2002). Hanushek and Rivkin (2004), summarizing their own and other research, came to the same conclusion.

A recent study by Aaronson et al. (2003) of Chicago public teachers illustrates this point well. Like other such studies, this work was based on a very large longitudinal file of linked student achievement scores. What makes this study unique is that the authors also had extensive administrative data on teacher characteristics that are unavailable in other studies, including education, experience, types of teaching licenses, and selectivity of

---

[6]A recent survey of teacher quality research by the Education Commission of the States (Allen, 2003) sets a lower standard for inclusion of studies. Allen considered cross-section as well as descriptive studies. Nonetheless, he found at best tepid research support for aggressive regulation of the teacher labor market. On the question of whether pedagogical training contributes to teacher effectiveness, he found only "limited" support in the research, and added "It is not clear from the research reviewed for this report, however, whether such knowledge and skills are best acquired through coursework, field experience (especially student teaching) or on the job" (p. 29). On the question of whether more stringent screening for teacher training program entrants pays off in terms of student achievement, he found the literature "inconclusive." A new study by Betts, Zau, and Rice (2003) examined student achievement gains in the San Diego school district. They found mixed results for teacher credentials. In some cases, students of emergency certified teachers have higher gains than those of experienced fully credentialed teachers. At the upper grade levels, full certification in math has a significant positive effect in high schools but a negative effect in middle schools.

the teacher's undergraduate college. They found that over 90% of teacher effects are not explained by any measured teacher characteristics.

In sum, the growing "teacher effects" literature suggests that teacher quality, as measured by student achievement gains, is highly idiosyncratic. This does not mean that teacher quality is random or unknowable. It simply means that traditional measures of teacher quality such as experience, master's degree, and education coursework explain virtually none of the variation in teacher effectiveness.[7]

In the Absence of Strong Ex Ante *Indicators of Teaching Quality, Raising the Bar in Teacher Licensing Is Likely to Lower Teacher Quality*

A skeptic might argue that, although the evidence for teacher licensing, testing, or a particular program of pedagogical training is weak, why not raise the entry bar anyway on the chance that that it might work? Many public policies are enacted on faith and good intentions rather than rigorous scientific research. Why is teacher licensing any different? What harm can come from raising the bar for teachers?

If these reforms were costless, then one might make the case for their implementation on the chance that some benefits would accrue. However, they are not costless, and there is a very real possibility that schools will find themselves worse off and student achievement will fall if such programs are implemented.

First, there are the direct resource costs. To the extent that we raise requirements for education coursework, we incur direct educational costs as candidates take classes, pursue professional development, forego other employment, and so forth. Annual costs per student in higher education currently are roughly $27,000 dollars per year, although students on average only pay part of this cost. Tests are less costly, but the fixed costs of updating and validating new teacher tests is considerable. More important are the time costs for teaching candidates spent in pedagogy courses or preparing for and taking exams. If we assume teaching candidates take 1½ years of teaching courses (including student teaching), this is a very costly investment. Even at the minimum wage, this amounts to over $15,000. One perverse result of requiring seat time in pedagogy courses for labor market entry is that candidates with greater academic skills, who presumably

---

[7]It may be that other potential measures, involving direct observation of classroom practice, or psychological assessments of teacher attitudes toward students and teaching may do a better job of explaining the classroom effectiveness. Indeed, many school districts use the latter types of assessments in their hiring decisions.

have a higher alternative wage, face a higher cost in securing a teaching license (Ballou & Podgursky, 1997).

Only roughly 60% of all teacher candidates graduate from NCATE-accredited teacher training programs. Closing all teacher training programs that do not secure NCATE accreditation, as proposed by the National Education Association and the NCTAF, would almost surely restrict the flow of newly trained teaching candidates. So, too, would raising the cutoff on teacher licensing exams. If the cutoff is raised from the 20th to the 30th percentile on elementary education exams, then 10% of potential applicants are excluded from the applicant pool.

A common feature of all of these policies is that they would reduce the applicant pool to public schools. Other things being equal, this will tend to lower the average quality of teachers who are hired. Why is this the case? School administrators know many things about teacher candidates that state regulators do not. They conduct job interviews, evaluate student teaching, read letters of recommendation and transcripts, and observe demonstration classes. In fact, school administrators are in a much better position to assess teacher quality than are state regulators, and there is some evidence that their assessments can identify teachers who produce larger student achievement gains.[8] By preventing school administrators from considering any unlicensed applicants, school districts are forced to hire the worst certified candidate even if a superior noncertified candidate is available. Raising the bar shrinks the size of the applicant pool that school administrations may consider. The new pool is better in terms of whatever the regulators specify (e.g., more NCATE graduates, higher Praxis II scores), but now the administrators have fewer candidates in the applicant pool. Therefore, they have less ability to select among candidates on the basis of the factors that they observe, but state regulators do not.

This cost of mandatory certification is illustrated in Figure 1. Here I have presented hypothetical data on the distribution of teacher quality among certified and uncertified applicants. Although these data are hypothetical, I believe that they represent the general picture that is emerging in the teacher effects literature—namely, that the individual variation in classroom performance of teachers is large relative to any measurable teacher characteristic such as teacher certification. As I indicated earlier, the evidence concerning teacher certification is mixed at best. However, for the sake of argument, I have assumed a positive effect: The average certified

---

[8]Studies using student longitudinal data by Armor et al. (1976) and Murnane (1975) find large effects of principal evaluations on student achievement gains. More recently, Sanders and Horn (1994) reported, "There is a very strong correlation between teacher effects as determined by the data and subjective evaluations by supervisors" (p. 300).

teacher is better than 60% of noncertified teachers. Based on the review of the research literature discussed earlier, I see this as an upper-end estimate for certification. However, the conclusions that follow do not hinge in any significant way on this assumption. If we bumped the assumption upward and had certified teachers better than 80% of potential candidates, none of our basic conclusions would change. The key point is that the research suggests that there is a large dispersion of quality within the certified and uncertified pools.

Suppose Figure 1 represents the population from which a school district recruits teaching candidates. Further suppose that the school district has a single vacancy and is free to hire the best candidate, certified or not. Imagine that a single candidate applies at random from the certified pool and one applies from the uncertified pool. What is the probability that the certified candidate is the superior teacher? In Table 1 we see that 57% of the time the certified candidate is better. With 2 job applicants, the average quality of the best teacher (certified or not) is at the 67th percentile of the certified distribution. Now suppose the school has 5 random applicants from the certified population but no uncertified applicants. Note that the quality of the best applicant jumps sharply from the 67th to the 88th percentile. This illustrates an important point. If teachers are screened well (a point taken up later), a larger applicant pool means better quality hires. The reason is that you are hiring the *best* applicant out of a pool, not the *average* applicant; therefore, it is better to have more rather than few appli-

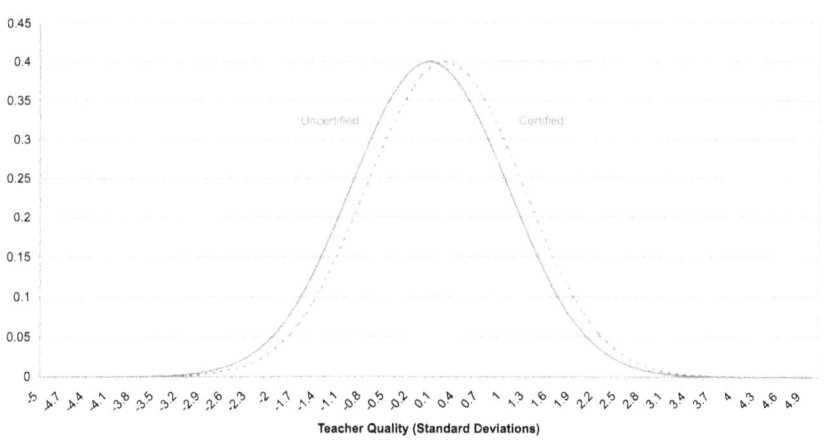

Figure 1. Overlapping ability when the average certified applicant is better than 60% of noncertified applicants.

Table 1

Probability That a Noncertified Candidate Is the Best Applicant

Applicant Pool	Probability That Certified Applicant Is Best Candidate in Pool	Average Quality of Best Applicant, Percentile of Certified Distribution
1 Certified 1 Uncertified	.57	67
5 Certified 0 Uncertified	1.00	88
5 Certified 5 Uncertified	.61	92

cants. This common sense point is borne out in many other contexts. Other things equal, the average quality of graduate students will be higher in a program with 200 applicants as compared to one with 20, even if the mean quality of the two applicant pools is the same.

Can this district similarly benefit from access to a pool of lower average quality uncertified applicants? The answer is yes (see bottom of Table 1). Here we suppose that 5 uncertified applicants are allowed to apply for the job along with 5 certified applicants. Although the uncertified applicants are of lower average quality than the certified candidates, 39% of the time the uncertified applicant will be the best of the 10 applicants. Why? The last column shows that by expanding the applicant pool from 5 to 10 candidates, the mean quality of the best teacher has increased as well. Raising the bar and restricting the applicant pool moves us in the opposite direction. If we go from row 3 with 10 applicants to row 2 with 5 applicants, average teacher quality falls despite the fact that the average certified teacher is better than the average noncertified teacher. The fall in mean teacher quality as we go from row 3 to row 2 illustrates the hidden cost of a licensing entry barrier: Shrinking the applicant pool gives schools fewer choices, gives them less freedom to pick out talent, and reduces the mean quality of the resulting hires.[9]

To summarize, raising the bar on teacher licensing shrinks the applicant pool available to schools. Other things being equal, this will tend to lower

---

[9] A skeptic might argue that I have "stacked the deck" in this simple simulation by assuming that in hiring the school district screens perfectly and always hires the best candidate. However, in a more elaborate simulation, Ballou (1999) assumed that school administrators have imperfect, but independent, information about the quality of job applicants (i.e., over and above certification or a test score). Such information might include direct observation of teaching, recommendations, or prior teaching experience. In that case, we find a similar result to the one we observe here. Ballou also showed that the cost of the reduced supply tends to be larger for low SES districts that tend to draw relatively more applicants around the cut scores.

the quality of the teaching workforce. This negative effect or cost may be offset if licensing raises the mean quality of the (smaller) applicant pool. However, the research to date provides little solid evidence for such a positive effect. Therefore, we are faced with the likelihood that mean teacher quality will actually decline as a result of such policies.[10]

Teaching Is Not Medicine

Whether or not a research base currently exists to support aggressive licensing of teacher labor markets, proponents often argue that teacher "professionalization" is a desirable end in itself. They appeal to a vision of professional self-regulation in education akin to that in medicine. In panel discussions on teacher licensing, I am routinely confronted with the question, "Would you send your children to an unlicensed doctor?" Although rarely stated explicitly, I believe the argument runs as follows: Although it may be true that there exists no rigorous evidence for the reforms we have proposed (e.g., tougher teacher testing, accreditation, and more vigorous review of teacher training institutions), they are broadly similar to what is found in medicine. Therefore, if we implement such reforms, teacher quality and the quality of education will improve in the manner seen in medicine.

Argument by analogy is valid only if the analogy is valid. Why teaching is not medicine deserves an entire article of its own; however, I briefly explain two important reasons why this analogy is inappropriate.

There is a deep body of scientific research in medicine, and commitment to scientific research methods pervades medical schools, the professional specialty associations, and the community of medical practitioners generally. The economic case for medical licensing rests on an information *asymmetry* between what these highly trained medical practitioners know and what consumers know concerning the quality of the services they are buying. Because of the complexity of the knowledge base in medicine and the high cost of mistakes (malpractice), it is relatively easy to argue that some sort of government licensing is required to screen out incompetent practitioners and protect consumers.

Does this model apply to K–12 education? If we replicate the professional self-regulation found in medicine, can we expect qualitatively similar outcomes in education? To be sure, there is scientifically based research on student learning. However, for the most part, this research is being produced not in schools of education but by educational and cognitive psychologists in psychology departments.

---

[10]Ballou (1999) showed that this negative net effect is more likely to occur in high-poverty districts where many teachers hired are near the cut scores on licensing exams.

Even at leading research universities, the majority of education school faculty do not produce research based on rigorous scientific methodology—certainly nothing akin to what one finds in a medical school. Many education faculty approach research with methods more akin to those found in the humanities than those in medicine or the sciences. Controlled experiments and randomized studies are rare. Use of large-scale longitudinal data on students is not widespread. However, what education school faculty at leading research universities do or do not do is largely irrelevant because they train relatively few of the nation's classroom teachers. The primary supplier of classroom teachers (as opposed to doctors) are state colleges—most of which were formerly teacher's colleges. At such institutions, much of the teaching is conducted by adjunct faculty not actively engaged in scientific research. To the extent that regular faculty at such institutions do research at all, it cannot be described as scientifically rigorous and is far removed from the frontiers of scientific research on human learning. The same can be said of other areas of education policy research.

However, even if upper and lower tier schools of education were producing scientifically based research, the teachers and their professional associations are in no position to vet this research and incorporate it into their teaching or their standards. Professional teacher associations such as the National Council of Teachers of English or the National Council of Social Studies do not base their standards on scientific research. Indeed, most members of these learned societies are practicing teachers and not trained to evaluate scientific research. I venture that most practitioners and education school professors in these fields would not even view the scientific method (i.e., experiments) as the most useful method of inquiry in their field.

The deep technical and scientific knowledge base in medicine produces well-defined and widely shared agreement on appropriate clinical practice. For the most part, this is absent in education. Although the judgment of English, mathematics, and elementary school teachers as to the best ways of teaching a subject certainly deserve respect and deference, there is little evidence to suggest that parents cannot make informed choices among practitioners who approach their craft differently.[11] This leads us to the next proposition.

---

[11] A recent paper by Angrist and Guryan (2003) found that states with teacher testing have higher teacher pay (indicating a restriction in supply) but no higher teacher quality as measured by various academic quality indicators (e.g., selective college graduates). Another subtle difference between teaching and medicine (as well as other professions) deserves mention. In medicine, the primary desire of a patient is simply to be made well. When we go to a doctor

Unregulated Markets in Education and Training Work Well

The case for the medical analogy would be strengthened if there were pervasive evidence of "market failure" in unregulated markets for education and training. Although I am not aware of widespread unlicensed practice of surgery, unlicensed training and schooling is pervasive in our economy. The latter markets seem to work quite well with little or no government regulation. In fact, a review of the functioning of these labor markets suggests that they operate considerably better than the highly regulated markets in public K–12 education.

Researchers have estimated that American business spends between $18 and $43 billion (1995 dollars) annually on formal training programs for their workers and an unknown but substantial amount on informal training (Ehrenberg & Smith, 1996, p. 302). Virtually all of this training is delivered by instructors who are not licensed by the state and who have not received specialized pedagogical instruction. Historically, one of the most important sources of high-quality vocational training in our economy has been the U.S. military. The various services have taken millions of high school dropouts and graduates and provided them with high-quality training in technical specialty fields. Along the way, in the process of turning millions of young men and women with limited elementary and secondary education into trained aircraft mechanics, radio operators, supply clerks, and so forth, the armed services have taught these young recruits basic literacy and numeracy skills as well. Nearly all of this was accomplished by unlicensed instructors.

with a ruptured appendix, a dentist with a toothache, or a lawyer for legal representation, we want a "sage on the stage," not a "guide at the side." That is, we want their professional expertise put to work solving our problem. Usually, the process is a secondary concern to the end, and we usually defer to the judgment of the expert professional on the best course of "treatment." Of course, if there are several ways to achieve the same end, the consumer will need to make a choice. However, more often than not, the treatment protocols are standard, and the consumer follows the advice of the doctor to achieve the desired end (a cure). However, in education, for many parents, the *process* is as important as the end result. Indeed, the two can be hard to separate. When parents choose a Montessori or a Waldorf school for their children, they clearly expect their children to learn basic literacy and numeracy skills, but they are also expressing a preference over a mode of inquiry and learning as well. Similarly, when parents object to the use of calculators by young children as in the initial National Council of Teachers of Mathematics standards or to whole language reading instruction, they are expressing a preference for a type of instruction as well as an outcome. In fact, the experience in the private K–12 education marketplace suggest that parents are perfectly capable of making informed choices among vendors who offer a wide range of instructional strategies (e.g., from constructivist, to traditional, to military schools) and can select a school that meets their preferences. We see little evidence of market failure or calls for government regulations coming from private school consumers.

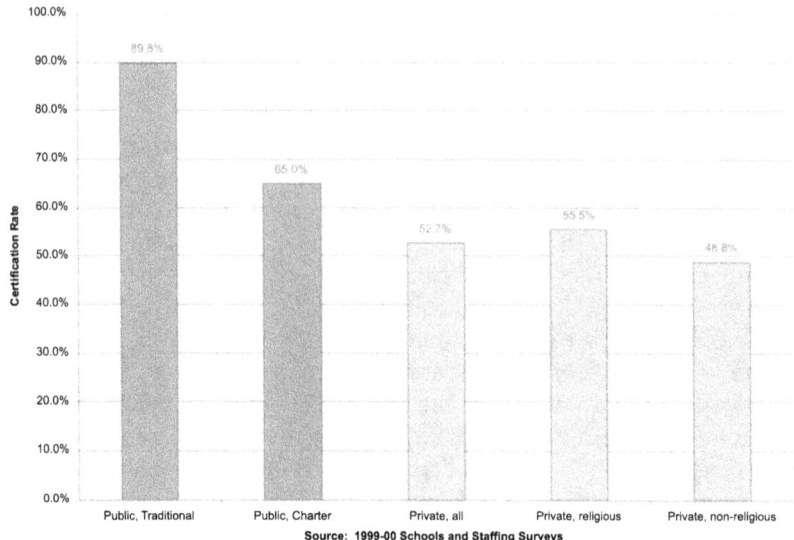

Figure 2. Percentage of teachers holding regular state certification in a primary teaching area: traditional public, private, and charter schools. Source: 1999–00 Schools and Staffing Surveys.

Approximately 6 million students are enrolled in 2-year community colleges. Much of the coursework offered in these community colleges is remedial and covers material that students should have learned in elementary and secondary schools. States do not require the faculty in community colleges to be licensed, and evidence suggests that most are not certified teachers. Nonetheless, if we judge success by enrollment growth, successful transition to 4-year baccalaureate institutions, or higher earnings, these community colleges are successfully delivering K–12 educational services.

Many students receive K–12 educational services from the thousands of private tutoring firms. These range from large multinational educational firms like Sylvan Learning to small independent proprietary firms. Many of these firms specialize in providing remedial help for students in reading and mathematics. Others, like Kaplan, focus on test preparation. In any event, these firms are selling K–12 educational services to the public. There are no state licensing requirements for teachers in these firms (or for the firms themselves), and all indications are that this market is expanding.

Finally, there is a thriving private K–12 school system in the United States that long predates the public school system. Private schools routinely hire unlicensed teachers. Figure 2 provides some data on certification rates of private school teachers. The dependent variable is whether the teacher holds regular or provisional state certification in her primary teaching area. The rate for the public sector is 89.8%, whereas the rate for private schools is much lower, particularly in nonreligious schools where just 48.8% of teachers are certified. The rates are lower still at the secondary level. In nonreligious secondary schools the certification rate is just 35.1%. Therefore, although private schools do hire certified teachers, they also hire substantial numbers of noncertified teachers as well. It should also be noted that charter schools, too, hire large numbers of uncertified teachers.

How does the academic quality of the uncertified teachers compare to that of the certified? One measure of teacher quality is the selectivity of the college from which the teacher graduated. Several production function studies find that the selectivity of a teacher's undergraduate college is correlated with student academic achievement (Ehrenberg & Brewer, 1993, 1994; Summers & Wolfe, 1977; Winkler, 1975). The data in Table 2 suggest that private schools use this flexibility to trade off teacher certification to get higher academic quality for teachers.[12] The share of teachers graduating from selective institutions, math and science majors, and academic majors is consistently higher in the noncertified population. A similar pattern is seen in charter schools. In other words, in terms of Figure 2, charter and private schools benefit from their ability to hire outside the certified candidate pool when an attractive noncertified applicant appears in the applicant pool.

State Teacher Licensing Systems Are so Complex That No One Is in Compliance Anyway

Proponents of raising the bar for teaching licenses assume that such proposals are feasible. However, I find that state licensing systems are already so complex that virtually no school district is in compliance anyway. This raises a serious question as to what we accomplish by raising bars.

Like all other states with which I am familiar, the state of Missouri issues a single license to practice medicine, law, dentistry, accounting, nursing, and veterinary medicine. However, in the area of K–12 education, the Missouri Department of Elementary and Secondary Education currently issues 260 certificates and endorsements (171 vocational, 89 nonvocational). However, that is only part of the story. There are levels of certification (permanent, provisional) for all of these and a host of "grandmothered" codes. As a consequence, there are 781 valid certification codes in the master teacher certification file. There is nothing unique about Missouri. Most other states have equally Byzantine systems for teacher licensing.

---

[12]Further evidence on differences in personnel policies between traditional public and private and charter schools is found in Ballou and Podgursky (1997) and Podgursky and Ballou (2001).

Table 2

Measures of Teacher Quality in Public and Private Schools

	Traditional Public: All	Public Charter		Private Religious		Private Nonreligious	
		Certified	Not Certified	Certified	Not Certified	Certified	Not Certified
College selectivity: Most competitive	0.9	1.4	4.0	0.8	3.1	3.4	9.4
Other selective	22.1	26.7	29.5	18.5	21.4	30.3	32.8
Total selective	23.0	28.1	33.5	19.3	24.5	33.7	42.2
Math and science majors	10.1	10.1	12.8	11.1	10.8	11.6	13.7
Academic majors	33.7	40.9	56.3	37.2	55.5	39.0	63.0

Note. Data from 1999–00 Schools and Staffing Surveys.

How is it that the public is protected by a single license in other professions, yet K–12 education requires over 100? Is teaching a more complex endeavor? I believe that part of the answer is that in these other professions licensing is simply used to screen out incompetent practitioners but is not meant to control how labor is utilized in that sector. After a practitioner enters the profession, he is free to specialize in any field he chooses. Most doctors do proceed to earn certification in 1 of the 24 medical specialties, but there is no state requirement that they do so. If a medical clinic chooses to use a neurosurgeon to treat walk-in family practice patients, there are no legal impediments to doing so. Once licensed, lawyers are free to practice any type of law they choose. One does not read about a crisis of lawyers "practicing law out of field," nurses "nursing out of field," or dentists engaged in "dentistry out of field."

In K–12 education, state regulators attempt to use the licensing system to control how teacher labor is allocated. The presumption is that local schools cannot be trusted to staff courses appropriately. Therefore, this complicated licensing system is the state's clumsy attempt to monitor the performance of local administrators. In Missouri, school districts are routinely audited to determine whether the hundreds of different types of courses taught match to the right certificate or endorsements for the teacher of record. If states issued a single license in teaching as in other professions, most of the out-of-field teaching that is the subject of so much hand wringing would disappear.

The excessively complex licensing system in K–12 education can also be seen as a means by which teacher unions and schools of education engage in "rent capture" (i.e., using government regulation to produce private pecuniary gains). To make the case for higher pay and benefits for their members, any type of supply restriction is desirable from the point of view of teacher unions, so long as the added restrictions apply to new entrants and not dues-paying incumbents. However, high standards for program entry, as in medicine, would invariably drive many schools of education out of business. Therefore, a compromise between the teacher unions and the schools of education is to proliferate certificate areas, generating more demand for education school courses but also restricting supply to school districts.

As a consequence of the complex licensing systems that states have constructed, virtually no school district in the United States is in full compliance. The complexity of the state licensing systems make national tabulations of unlicensed, uncertified, or substandard certification difficult. Therefore, I illustrate this point with administrative data from two states. Figure 3 presents data for Missouri public K–12 school districts (I have excluded K–8 districts). On the vertical axis we measure the percentage of courses taught by teachers with inappropriate licenses during the 2001–02

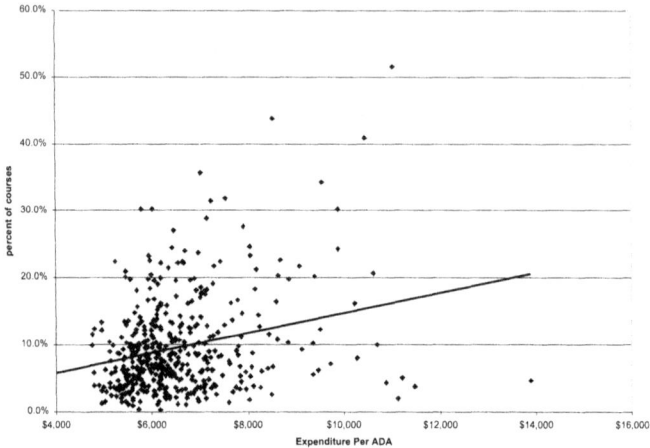

Figure 3. Percentage of courses taught by teachers with inappropriate or no licenses by expenditure per pupil in average daily attendance: Missouri K–12 public school districts, 2001–02. Source: Missouri Department of Elementary and Secondary Education.

school year. On the horizontal axis we measure spending per student in average daily attendance. Of 447 K–12 school districts, not a single district had no courses taught by an inappropriately licensed teacher (the average was 9.5%). Moreover, the prevalence of inappropriate licensed practice seems to have little to do with school revenues. The correlation between the rate of unlicensed teaching and spending per student is positive and statistically significant (.27).

My second example is decidedly nonrandom. Westchester County, New York, is home to some of the wealthiest households and highest paid schoolteachers in the United States. The schools in these exclusive communities are appropriately compared to the very best private day schools. In Figure 4, I have plotted percentage of uncertified teachers and median teacher salaries for school year 2000–01 from the most recent report of the New York State Department of Education. (*Uncertified* means the percentage of classroom teachers who teach more than 20% of their time in a subject or subjects for which they hold no certification or emergency license.) Despite very high salaries, no district in Westchester County has fewer than 2% of their teachers uncertified. Note that Scarsdale, which boasted a 2000–01 median teacher salary of $90,191, had 6% of its teachers uncertified. (As a regular reader of the *New York Times*, I have yet to read about Scarsdale parents complaining about the quality of their uncertified teachers.) If not a single school district in what may be the highest spending county in the United States is in full compliance with the New York State

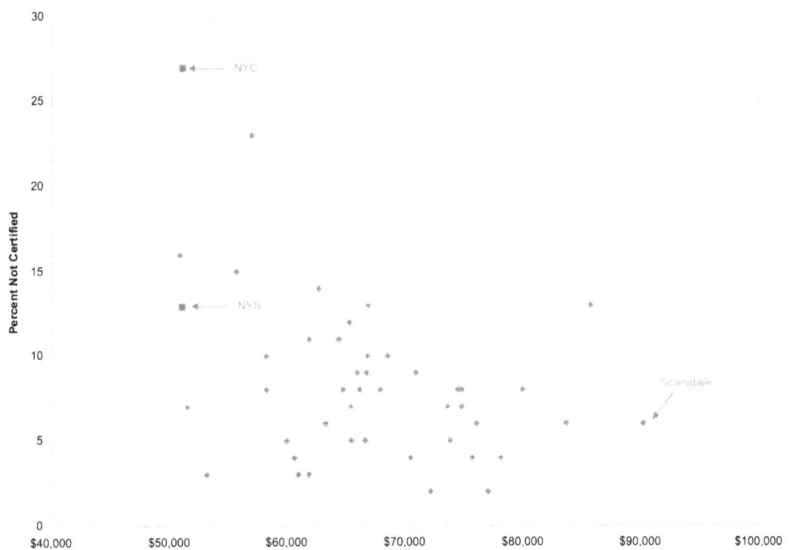

Figure 4. Percentage of teachers not certified and median salaries in Westchester County, New York, public school districts: 2000–01. Source: New York State Department of Education.

law, this raises serious questions as to how we can contemplate raising the bar on teacher licensing.

The Model

In light of the six propositions laid out in the previous section, the case for a more flexible licensing model is relatively straightforward. State education regulators should protect the public by focusing on what they can measure (student learning) and not on what they cannot (teacher quality). That is, they should focus on education outputs rather than education inputs. As noted earlier, research to date suggests that teacher quality as measured by student learning is idiosyncratic and not well measured by anything that state regulators are in a position to monitor. Local school administrators, on the other hand, are in a good position to monitor teacher classroom performance. Therefore, the model that emerges has several features.[13]

The first, and most important, is getting incentives right. Local administrators must be held accountable for student learning, and state regula-

---

[13]The model proposed here is similar to that in Hess (2001), which he described as "competitive certification."

tors need to focus their attention on monitoring student learning. Nearly all states have developed standards for what students should be learning at various grade levels and assessments of the learning that are actually occurring by grade in schools and districts. These data are now routinely provided to parents and to the public at large. Schools that demonstrate persistently poor performance in terms of student learning increasingly face administrative sanctions. Another important mechanism for producing accountability is school choice. Indeed, one of the most important protections for parents against incompetent teachers is to give them the option to choose another classroom or school if their assigned teacher fails.

If a school accountability regime is in place with information on performance widely available, with state monitoring of school performance, and with parental choice of schools, the role of the state in monitoring "teacher quality"—something that they cannot measure anyway—should whither away. As far as teacher licensing is concerned, the guiding principal for the state should be a simple "do no harm" standard. Certainly, teachers should undergo a careful criminal background check. Current bureaucratic impediments to removing teachers who have been convicted or indicted for serious criminal offenses should be removed. It is reasonable that teachers should also be required to hold a bachelor's degree.

Tests of general academic knowledge and subject matter knowledge are reasonable. However, as noted earlier, it is likely to be counterproductive for states to set high cut scores for these exams. A more attractive approach (which is likely to survive legal challenge) is to set relatively low cut scores and provide information on the candidate's scores to the school districts. From an economic point of view, the current system makes little sense. Teacher candidates may spend hundreds of dollars taking licensing exams. The testing companies then take these continuous test scores and collapse them into a "pass" or "fail" grade. That is the only result that school districts ever see. Large testing companies such as the Educational Testing Service will not provide these exam scores to school districts. Indeed, they make the tenuous argument that the scores only have "validity" for licensing but not for hiring. Imagine if colleges or professional schools received similar information. Continuous SAT or GRE scores would be collapsed into binary pass or fail measures indicating that a student was "good enough for graduate study" or "not good enough for graduate study." The test scores would have "validity" only for determining who can enter the market for graduate study but not for the admissions decisions of any graduate program. Academics would immediately dismiss such a proposal as absurd; yet, somehow this type of reasoning holds sway in occupational licensing.

Of course, providing flexibility for schools to audition many candidates means that schools must have the ability to act on that information. In fact, in most states school districts have considerable leeway to not rehire teachers during an initial probationary period of 2 to 5 years. After that, once teachers are "tenured," or enjoy the right of automatic contract renewal, it becomes very costly to dismiss teachers for anything but the most negligent job performance. Sensible reforms would make it easier to not renew the contracts of ineffective senior teachers.

Even if a "magic bullet" in terms of teacher training or testing were found, it would be many years before new, more effective teachers diffuse through the teaching workforce. Teacher turnover averages roughly 6% to 8% annually, and about one half of new teacher hires are returning teachers or interdistrict transfers (Broughman & Rollefson, 2000). Therefore, only a very small share of teachers are affected by licensing reform in any year. Schools have information on the job performance of 90% of job candidates who do not turn over. They need the flexibility and incentives to use this performance information in personnel matters, including pay and contract renewal.

To summarize, the most efficient flexible regime would have the following features:

- Accountability for student learning through testing, sanctions, and parental choice.
- State regulators who actively promote a competitive market in teacher quality and protect schools from anticompetitive practices on the part of teacher unions, schools of education, or other education producer organizations.
- Minimal state licensing standards for teachers: criminal background check, bachelor's degree, test of general and content knowledge.
- Full information on teacher test results provided to school administrators.
- Award of a permanent or full license on the basis of successful job performance.

Statutory Changes

State boards or professional certification boards generally have considerable discretion as to the content and requirements for teaching licenses. There is certainly ample precedent for a flexible policy. Many states have now created alternative routes to teacher certification that provide a good model for what I have proposed. The Alternative Certification Program in Texas and the Intern Program in California are examples. In such programs, prospective teachers must hold a bachelor of arts degree, pass exams, and demonstrate content knowledge to receive a probationary license. After a probationary period of 2 to 3 years (which in these states includes on-site or off-site professional development), mentored practice, and satisfactory evaluations by supervisors, the teachers receive a standard license (Feistritzer, 2003). Such alternate route teachers satisfy the highly qualified teacher requirement of the No Child Left Behind Act.

Role of Education Schools and Organizations

Some years ago, Myron Lieberman (1993) perceptively described the K–12 education industry as "producer dominated." I find this description accurate, particularly in the area of teacher training and licensing where education school faculty and teacher organizations dominate the regulatory process. Both the teacher unions and the education schools have a common interest in "professionalizing" teaching by restricting supply through proliferation of certificates and suppressing competition in teacher training (e.g., by preventing entry by new institutions). Moreover, I also find a similar view in state education departments, which embrace "teacher professionalization" as part of their mission along with raising student achievement.

Moving to the flexible model described earlier would create strong competitive pressures for teacher training organizations to improve. Simply put, if education school courses are no longer required to hold a teaching license, then the monopoly power of schools of education largely disappears. If the pedagogical training offered by schools of education does, in fact, raise student achievement, then graduates from such programs will enjoy a competitive edge in the labor market and have more desirable job offers than their untrained peers. In that case, students will flock to such programs. On the other hand, if a teacher training program cannot attract adequate enrollments in a market in which job candidates and employers have flexibility as to the credentials, then it will go out of business. Effective programs will thrive and ineffective programs will whither away.

Any institution, public or private, would be free to enter the market and provide teacher training. If a history department at a small liberal arts college wanted to train teachers by offering a course preparing majors to teach in secondary schools and worked out student teaching arrangements with nearby schools, they would be free to do so. Unlike the current system, they would not be required to "partner" with a school of education.

When a major bank comes to a university campus to recruit candidates for management positions, they can interview finance majors in the business school, economics majors in the College of Arts and Sciences, or operations research or computer science majors from the engineering school. There are no licensing entry barriers creating a monopoly for a particular college. Opening up the teacher training market to competition is a more effective way to "fix" the quality problem in schools of education than regulation by state departments of education or mandatory accreditation by NCATE. It is common knowledge that low-quality schools of education have succeeded in securing approval from state education agencies as well as accreditation from NCATE. Clearly, both of these quality control systems have failed to weed out programs with academically mediocre students or low pass rates on state licensing examinations.

Finally, a flexible regime will require some change in gestalt among the regulators in state education agencies. The primary objective of state regulators should be increasing student learning and narrowing achievement gaps. How schools and districts do this—assuming the behavior is ethical and legal—should be of secondary importance. Children are protected from incompetent practice by monitoring learning through regular testing and by school choice.

On the other hand, state education agencies should not be in the business of promoting teacher professionalism. Here is where a change of gestalt is required. Promoting teacher professionalism is a role for private organizations. If organizations like teacher unions and (private or public) schools of education choose to promote teacher professionalization by securing accreditation of teacher training programs by NCATE, that is their choice. However, state education agencies should not impose these choices on the entire market through manipulation of licensing requirements.

Moreover, it should be recognized that in some educational endeavors, the most cost-efficient way to promote student achievement might involve *de-professionalization* of teaching. In some schools or programs, highly scripted curricula, distance learning, or computer-based instructional programs may reduce the need for highly trained teachers. Schools should face incentives to adopt the most cost-efficient approaches to promoting student learning, whether they advance teacher professionalization. If in the name of teacher professionalization state education agencies encourage schools to spend additional resources when more cost-effective means for instructional delivery are available, then resources that might have been used to lower class sizes or otherwise enhance student welfare have been diverted. In fact, it may be the case that the resources saved on teachers might more effectively promote student learning outside of K–12 schools (e.g., in better medical care for poor women, reduction of crime and drugs in low-income communities, or preschool care).

Should states continue to regulate teacher training programs? Because there is virtually no reliable research establishing a causal link between any program of teacher training and student achievement gains, state regulators have little basis for regulating teacher training programs. Some states and federal legislation (Title 2 of the Higher Education Act, P.L. 105–244, 1998) have focused on pass rates on teacher licensing exams as one criterion to judge programs. In my own analysis of Missouri data, I have found that the most important predictor of whether a teacher passes a Praxis II exam is his or her American College Test (ACT) score. Once we control for student ACT scores, there are few significant differences between institutions. In addition, there is wide dispersion of test scores within any institution. If pass rates primarily reflect the academic ability of the students entering the teacher training program, it makes little sense to use pass rates to assess the quality of a training program.

Because there is no reliable research base for approving or denying a teacher training program, and institutional pass rates are largely driven by the quality of program entrants, a reasonable approach would be for regulators to be fairly liberal in program approval. The primary mechanism to raise program quality would be market pressures and not regulation. If a training program does a poor job of preparing teachers to meet state education standards, graduates from such programs will receive fewer job offers in the market and enrollments will decline. Eventually, the program may leave the market altogether. By the same token, programs that produce high-quality teachers will attract many applicants and expand.

In sum, state education agencies should create strong incentives for schools and districts to raise student achievement and give them flexibility as to how to they get the job done. If one or another model of professionalism promoted by private organizations is a cost-effective way for schools to achieve this end, then professionalization will expand. If it does not, then it will languish. However, this is not a matter of public policy.

Evaluation

Effective educational policy requires that educational interventions be evaluated. We find ourselves in the current situation precisely because the education research community has for decades failed to conduct research on teacher quality that meets scientific research standards. However, relaxing licensing standards will generate nonexperimental data on the causal relation between teacher credentials and student achievement. Ironically, the current system, by encouraging homogeneity, reduces our ability to assess teacher effects. If all teachers in a school district matriculate from the same teacher-training program, then it is impossible to estimate the effect of that program on student achievement. The best way to assess the effect of a treatment variable on an outcome variable is to maximize variation of the treatment variable. Relaxing entry barriers will generate much more natural variation in the workforce in the credentials and training of teachers. This will permit better evaluation of the effects of teacher credentials and training.

It is interesting to note that one factor that has often been ignored in the research literature on teacher certification has been the effect of the regulatory regime on the distribution of teaching certificates (i.e., What was the process that produced the observed distribution of teaching credentials?).

Consider the effect of emergency licenses or waivers. In the current regime, school districts are not supposed to hire such teachers if certified teachers are available. Therefore, the data we observe on teachers with emergency versus full licenses is generated by a process in which head-to-head competition between certified and noncertified teachers as depicted in Figure 2 is not permitted. It may be that in a more competitive regime, teachers with emergency licenses would be of higher quality. Why would this be? If schools were free to recruit emergency certified teachers in the same way that they recruit licensed teachers, many who do not currently pursue teaching jobs might be enticed to apply. The result would be a much larger pool of talented emergency candidates. With a larger pool from which to choose, those hired would presumably be of higher quality. As noted earlier, on average, schools will end up with a better hire if they have 50 applicants for a job than if they have 5.

What Could Go Wrong?

Does this approach involve risk? Yes, it does. Relaxing entry restrictions into teaching will permit greater flexibility for schools to seek out the best teachers and meet the performance targets set by state regulators. Regulators would protect parents and children against incompetent practice by monitoring student learning and making such data widely available. Parents would also be empowered to protect their children from poor teachers by giving them more choices among schools. Markets and competition are ultimately the best guarantor of quality in the provision of almost any service.

However, would such a system produce greater exposure of children to incompetent teachers? Ultimately, this is an empirical point; however, I do not believe that most objective observers of current licensing systems would argue that it is particularly effective in screening out incompetent practitioners. Indeed, as an empirical matter, it is likely the case the greatest harm from incompetent teacher practice comes not from novices but rather from experienced, licensed teachers who are protected by tenure statues.

Conclusion: The Tail Is Wagging the Dog

Policy debates about teacher quality have tended to dwell on teacher training and licensing. However, there is little research indicating that the types of licenses that teachers hold or the type of pedagogical training program they have passed through have a significant relation to student performance. However, even if effective changes in licensing or training were identified, it would be many years before significant effects on student achievement would be obtained. This is because the number of inexperienced teachers hired in any year is very small relative to the stock of incumbent or experienced teachers (Broughman & Rollefson, 2000). In other markets, the best we expect from licensing is to screen out incompetent new practitioners. However, the quality or performance for incumbents is primarily determined by incentives: Experienced dentists who do a poor job on our teeth lose customers; those who perform incompetently get sued.

I have argued that attempts to address the teacher quality problem by raising bars in teacher licensing are likely to make things worse rather than better. Because there is so little reliable research to guide setting criteria for market entry, and such modest effects of teacher credentials in the current research, all such approaches are likely to accomplish is a reduction in the size of the teacher applicant pool with little change in the average productivity of the applicants. However, in a world of uncertain teacher productivity, it is in the interest of school districts to have more candidates to audition than fewer.

A more productive approach is for state regulators to focus on what they can measure (student achievement) and not on what they cannot (teacher quality). State regulators should make sure local school administrators have adequate instructional resources and strong incentives for raising school performance. They should use licensing to reduce the likelihood that a demonstrably incompetent teacher is put into the classroom. A prudent standard in this regard is a test of general academic skills, and more specialized tests covering the teaching fields and subjects to which the teacher is assigned. However, the most important role for teacher licensing reform is permissive or enabling. We need to make sure that these procrustean licensing systems do not stand in the way of entrepreneurial school administrators who are responding to the incentives we create for improving student performance.

Rather than dwell on the credentials and training of the 3% to 4% newly minted teachers hired each year, it is much more important to create strong performance incentives for the other 95% of teachers. Performance incentives are absent when pay is set by rigid salary schedules and tenure systems that protect teachers whose poor performance warrants dismissal. Rather than expend further resources seeking indirect measures of job performance, such as licensing exam scores or teaching portfolios, it would be far more productive to make better use of available information on teaching performance for the 95% of incumbent teachers. Dismissing 2% of the least productive teachers in the workforce based on current job performance would surely have a much larger effect on student achievement than marginal changes in the training or licensing of 3% to 4% of newly minted hires. Finally, it is important to address the role that collective bargaining contracts play in stifling efforts to raise teacher quality, particularly in urban school districts.

Teacher quality and effort primarily is a management problem, not a licensing problem. School principals in major urban districts often lack the ability to select their teachers, dismiss ineffective teachers, and are often severely hampered by collective bargaining agreements (and licensing regulations) in how they can assign their teachers or staff vacant positions. With district-wide salary schedules, school administrators have a passive role in setting individual teacher pay. The teacher quality policy debate needs to focus on creating efficient incentive structures and reducing constraints on effective management. Teacher licensing is of secondary importance.

References

Aaronson, D., Barrow, L., & Sander, W. (2003, February). *Teachers and student achievement in the Chicago public high schools* (Working Paper No. 2002–28). Chicago: Federal Reserve Bank of Chicago.

Allen, M. B. (2003). *Eight questions on teacher pay: What does the research say?* Denver, CO: Education Commission of the States.

Angrist, J., & Guryan, J. (2003, March). *Does teacher testing raise teacher quality? Evidence from state certification measurements* (Working Paper No. 9545). Cambridge, MA: National Bureau of Economic Research.

Armor, D., Conry-Osenguera, P., Cox, M., King, N., McDonnell, L., Pascal, A., et al. (1976). *Analysis of the School Preferred Reading Program in selected Los Angeles minority schools*. Santa Monica, CA: Rand.

Ballou, D. (1999). *Recruiting smarter teachers: Is testing the answer?* Unpublished manuscript, Vanderbilt University, Nashville, TN.

Ballou, D., & Podgursky, M. (1997). *Teacher pay and teacher quality*. Kalamazoo, MI: W.E. Upjohn Institute for Employment Research.

Ballou, D., & Podgursky, M. (2000). Reforming teacher preparation and licensing: What does the evidence show? *Teacher College Record, 101*, 5–26.

Betts, J. R., Zau, A. C., & Rice, L. A. (2003). *Determinants of student achievement: New evidence from San Diego*. San Francisco: Public Policy Institute of California. Retrieved from http://www.ppic.org/content/pubs/R_803JBR.pdf

Broughman, S. P., & Rollefson, M. R. (2000). *Teacher supply in the United States: Sources of newly-hired teachers in public and private schools, 1987-88 to 1993-94*. Washington, DC: National Center for Education Statistics 2000-309.

Darling-Hammond, L. (2003). *Access to quality teaching: An analysis of inequality in California public schools*. Retrieved from http://www.mofo.com/decentschools/expert_reports/darling-hammond_report.pdf

Decker, P., Mayer, D., & Glazerman, S. (2004). *The effects of Teach for America on students: Findings from a national evaluation* (Tech. Rep. No. 8792-750). Princeton, NJ: Mathematica Policy Research.

Ehrenberg, R. C., & Brewer, D. J. (1993). Did teachers' race and verbal ability matter in the 1960's? Coleman revised. *Economics of Education Review, 14*(1), 1–23.

Ehrenberg, R. C., & Brewer, D. J. (1994). Do school and teacher characteristics matter? Evidence from high school and beyond. *Economics of Education Review, 13*(1), 1–17.

Ehrenberg, R. C., & Smith, R. S. (1996). *Modern labor economics* (6th ed.). Reading, MA: Addison-Wesley.

Feistritzer, E. C. (2003). *Alternative teacher certification: A state-by-state analysis: 1998–99*. Washington, DC: National Center for Education Information.

Goldhaber, D., & Brewer, D. J. (1997a). Evaluating the effect of teacher degree level on educational performance. In W. J. Fowler (Ed.), *Developments in school finance 1996* (pp. 197–210). Washington, DC: National Center for Education Statistics.

Goldhaber, D., & Brewer, D. J. (1997b). Why don't schools and teacher's seem to matter? *Journal of Human Resources, 32*, 505–523.

Goldhaber, D. (2002). The mystery of good teaching. *Education Next, 2*, 50–55.

Hanushek, E. A., & Rivkin, S. G. (2004). How to improve the supply of high-quality teachers. In D. Ravitch (Ed.), *Brookings papers on education policy: 2004* (pp. 7–44). Washington, DC: Brookings Institution Press.

Heckman, J. J., LaLonde, R. J., & Smith, J. A. (1999). The economics and econometrics of active labor market programs. In O. Ashenfelter & D. Card (Eds.), *Handbook of labor economics* (pp. 1865–2097). Amsterdam: Elsevier Science.

Hess, F. M. (2001). *Tear down this wall: The case for radical overhaul of teacher certification*. Washington, DC: Progressive Policy Institute.

Higher Education Act of 1965, Amendments, Pub. L. No. 105-224 (1998).

Hoxby, C. (2001). If families matter most, where do schools come in? In T. M. Moe (Ed.), *A primer on America's schools* (pp. 89–126). Stanford, CA: Hoover Institution Press, Stanford University.

Jacob, B. A., & Lefgren, L. (2002). *The impact of teacher training on student achievement: Quasi-experimental evidence from school reform efforts in Chicago* (Working Paper No. 8916). Cambridge, MA: National Bureau of Economic Research.

Lieberman, M. (1993). *Public education: An autopsy*. Cambridge, MA: Harvard University Press.

Mosteller, F., & Boruch, R. (Eds.). (2002). *Randomized trials in education research*. Washington, DC: Brookings Institution Press.

Murnane, R. (1975). *The impact of school resources on the learning of inner city children*. Cambridge, MA: Ballinger.

National Commission on Teaching and America's Future. (1996). *What matters most*. New York: Columbia University Press.

National Commission on Teaching and America's Future. (1997). *Doing what matters most*. New York: Columbia University Press.

No Child Left Behind Act of 2001, Pub. L. No. 107-110, 115 Stat. 1425 (2002).

Podgursky, M., & Ballou, D. (2001). *Personnel policy in charter schools.* Washington, DC: Thomas B. Fordham Foundation.

Ravitch, D. (1998, February 25). Put teachers to the test. *The Washington Post.* Retrieved from http://www.edexcellence.net/foundation/publication/publication.cfm?id=223

Rivkin, S. G., Hanushek, E. A., & Kain, J. F. (1998). *Teachers, schools, and academic achievement.* Unpublished manuscript.

Sanders, W. L., & Horn, S. P. (1994) The Tennessee Value-Added Assessment System (TVAAS): Mixed model methodology in educational assessment. *Journal of Personnel Evaluation in Education, 8,* 299–311.

Summers, A. M., & Wolfe, B. L. (1977). Do schools make a difference? *American Economic Review, 67,* 639–652.

U.S. Department of Education, Institute of Education Sciences. (n.d.). *Random assignment in program evaluation and intervention research: Questions and answers.* Retrieved from http://www.mathematica-mpr.com/PDFs/randomassign.pdf

Walsh, K. (2004) A candidate-centered model for teacher licensure. In F. Hess, A. J. Rotherham, & K. Walsh (Eds.), *A qualified teacher in every classroom? Appraising old answers and new ideas* (pp. 223–254). Cambridge, MA: Harvard Educational Press.

Winkler, D. R. (1975). Educational achievement and school peer group composition. *Journal of Human Resources, 10,* 189–204.

How Teaching Conditions Predict Teacher Turnover in California Schools

Susanna Loeb and Linda Darling-Hammond
School of Education
Stanford University

John Luczak
Program Officer for Education
Joyce Foundation

A number of studies have found that teachers are prone to leave schools serving high proportions of low-achieving, low-income, and minority students for more economically and educationally advantaged schools. In schools with very high turnover rates, this can pose a number of challenges, including lack of continuity in instruction, lack of adequate teaching expertise for making curriculum decisions and providing support and mentoring, and lost time and resources for replacement and training. If high rates of turnover are caused largely by student characteristics, then policy strategies to correct the problem are limited. However, due to data constraints, little research has sought to disentangle the effects of student demographic factors from occupational factors such as salaries and working conditions that may also influence turnover and are amenable to policy interventions. Using California teacher survey data linked to district data on salaries and staffing patterns, this study examines a range of school conditions as well as demographic factors and finds that high levels of school turnover are strongly affected by poor working conditions and low salaries, as well as by student characteris-

Requests for reprints should be sent to Susanna Loeb, 234 CERAS, 520 Galvez Mall, Stanford, CA 94305. E-mail: sloeb@stanford.edu

tics. Although schools' racial compositions and proportions of low-income students predict teacher turnover, salaries and working conditions—including large class sizes, facilities problems, multitrack schools, and lack of textbooks—are strong and significant factors in predicting high rates of turnover. Furthermore, when these conditions are taken into account, the influence of student characteristics on turnover is substantially reduced.

Much attention has recently focused on labor market variables that contribute to students' differential access to well-qualified teachers in schools serving more and less advantaged populations of students (Lankford, Loeb, & Wyckoff, 2002; National Commission on Teaching and America's Future [NCTAF], 1996, 2003). Along with issues associated with teacher recruitment are factors that influence decisions to leave the profession or to transfer among schools. Some analysts have argued that quit and transfer decisions are the largest component of teacher supply problems, as the lion's share of attrition stems from nonretirement choices (Ingersoll, 2001; NCTAF, 2003). The factors associated with these decisions, in the aggregate, are particularly important to understand in the case of schools with high rates of turnover, where the combined effects of individual quit decisions can be particularly problematic for school stability, curriculum coherence, instructional quality, and efficient use of resources (Shields et al., 2001).

Wages and benefits, nonpecuniary features such as working conditions and student body characteristics, and aspects of preparation and skill that influence teachers' success in the classroom are all likely to influence the decision to leave a school or to leave the occupation (Boyd, Lankford, Loeb, & Wyckoff, in press). A number of studies have looked at the influence of salaries on teacher decisions to leave teaching, and a few have looked at working conditions. Studies of school leavers have found that teachers leave schools with larger proportions of low-income and minority students at higher rates than other schools (Shen, 1997). Some research tracking patterns of transfers finds that teachers transfer out of high-minority schools into schools with fewer minority students (e.g., Carroll, Reichardt, & Guarino, 2000; Scafidi, Sjoquist, & Stinebrickner, 2002) and out of low-performing schools into better performing ones (Hanushek, Kain, & Rivkin, 2004).[1]

Given the confluence of negative schooling conditions in schools serving low-income and minority students, a critical issue for policymakers is

---

[1]However, two studies using earlier panel data (Heyns, 1988, and Stinebrickner, 1998, both using a national longitudinal data set, NLS–72) found that teachers did not leave schools serving low-income students at higher rates. In addition, Theobald (1990) found that Washington teachers in districts with high property values tended to leave the profession at higher rates. This, however, could include urban districts that serve low-income students.

whether these demographic variables can be disentangled from other factors that are amenable to policy influences. In this article we consider evidence concerning a number of these factors as they influence rates of school-level turnover, with an eye to what might be alterable through policy and practice. Whereas attrition in general may be a positive or negative occurrence for a school, depending on who leaves and for what reasons, high rates of turnover that undermine continuity in instruction and reflect difficulty securing or keeping competent teachers are problematic for school operations and for student achievement. Particularly, we focus on the organizational predictors of high attrition rates in schools where turnover is a major problem and vacancies are difficult to fill. We also use far more detailed data on school conditions than those found in previous studies of the effect of working conditions on decisions to quit or transfer.

Occupational Factors Influencing Turnover

Salaries

Substantial evidence suggests that wages play a role in retaining as well as attracting teachers. Baugh and Stone (1982), for example, found that teachers are at least as responsive to wages in their decision to enter teaching as are workers in other occupations. Studies employing national data sets and state administrative data have found that teachers are more likely to quit or transfer when they work in districts with lower wages, especially relative to alternative wage opportunities (Boe, Bobbitt, Cook, Whitener, & Weber, 1997; Brewer, 1996; Mont & Rees, 1996; Murnane, Singer, & Willett, 1989; Shen, 1997; Stinebrickner, 1998; Theobald, 1990; Theobald & Gritz, 1996).

Murnane and Olsen (1990), using data on North Carolina teachers who began teaching in 1975, found that a $1,000 increase in each salary step of a district's salary schedule would increase the teacher's mean duration in that district by 2 to 3 years. Teachers in high-demand fields like mathematics and science that have higher wage alternatives were especially vulnerable to salary differences in their decisions to remain in teaching. Hanushek, Kain, and Rivkin (1999) found, using Texas panel data on teachers and students, that increasing teacher salaries within a district by 10% reduces the probability of a teacher leaving the district by 2% for a teacher with 0 to 2 years of experience and by 1% for a teacher with 3 to 5 years of experience. Theobald (1990) and Gritz and Theobald (1996) found similar trends in retention linked to district and state wage levels for a sample of Washington State teachers, with the effects of salary differentials higher at the start of the teaching career. Using a national longitudinal data set (NLS–72), Stinebrickner (1998) found that a teacher receiving a wage about 1 *SD* above the mean would have a 9% greater probability of staying in teaching more than 5 years than a teacher earning the mean wage.

Working Conditions

Although there is less research about the effects of working conditions on teachers' quit decisions, there is evidence from surveys of teachers that working conditions play a role in decisions to leave teaching. The 1995 Schools and Staffing Surveys (SASS) Teacher Followup Survey found that attrition rates were higher in high-poverty than low-poverty schools, and those who left high-poverty schools were more than twice as likely as those in low-poverty schools to report leaving because of dissatisfaction with teaching (Darling-Hammond, 1997). The major areas of dissatisfaction ranged from student motivation and discipline to lack of administrative supports. Salaries were also a factor, but a less prominent one.

These school-level differences are not surprising because there are large variations in teachers' salaries and working conditions across schools. In 1994, not only were the best paid teachers in low-poverty schools earning over 35% more than the best paid teachers in high-poverty schools (National Center for Education Statistics [NCES], 1997a, Figure 6.2), they also experienced much easier working conditions including smaller class sizes and pupil loads and much more control over decision making in their schools (NCES, 1997a, Table A 4.15). Teachers in high-poverty schools were much less likely to say that they had influence over decisions concerning curriculum, texts, materials, or teaching policies. They were also much less likely to be satisfied with their salaries or to feel they had the necessary materials available to them to do their job (Darling-Hammond, 1997).

Using the 1994 SASS data, Weiss (1999) found that, after controlling for teachers' personal and educational backgrounds, teaching fields, salary, and class sizes, teachers' perceptions of professional working conditions—such as administrative support, availability of necessary materials, participation in decision making, and collegial opportunities—were the most significant predictor of beginning teachers' morale, career choice commitment, and plans to stay in teaching. Shen's (1997) analysis of the SASS follow-up surveys confirmed that teachers who left teaching or transferred schools not only had lower salaries, they also felt they had significantly less influence over school policies and that their problems were less well understood by their administrators.

A few studies have modeled the effect of school resources on teacher retention. Stinebrickner (1998) found only a small effect of student–teacher ratios on length of spells in teaching (in the expected direction but statistically insignificant); however, Theobald (1990) found that extremely large pupil:staff ratios are detrimental to staff retention. Theobald and Gritz (1996) found that male teachers are less likely to transfer to another school when they are in districts that spend more for teaching materials, suggesting that better resourced districts may have more holding power.

These few studies exploring individual teacher quit decisions shed some light on the relation between selected working conditions and teacher attrition but provide only spotty evidence about how a range of conditions may be related to school turnover rates. Moreover, although differences in teaching conditions and working conditions across school types have been documented, their implications for teacher attrition have not been systematically examined. Finally, previous studies documenting the influences of student characteristics such as race, class, and achievement on school turnover rates have not simultaneously examined a range of working conditions and salaries—conditions that may co-determinate with student characteristics—and that may also influence the holding power of schools.

The Problems of High-Turnover Schools

The conditions that create attrition in schools with high turnover may be distinctive. Teacher turnover—including both "movers," who leave one school or district for another; and "leavers," who exit the profession temporarily or permanently—is 50% higher in high-poverty than in low-poverty schools (Ingersoll, 2001, p. 516), and new teachers in urban districts exit or transfer at higher rates than their suburban counterparts (Hanushek et al., 1999). The end result is that some of these schools are staffed disproportionately with inexperienced and often untrained teachers.

In a set of studies regarding teacher quality in California, Stanford Research Institute researchers used a benchmark of 20% or more teachers without clear credentials to demarcate schools that have "high concentrations" of underqualified teachers, arguing that such high levels "can create problems throughout the entire school community" (Shields et al., 1999, p. 47; see also Shields et al., 2001). These problems include high turnover of untrained teachers, which creates continual hiring needs and instability; a lack of mentors, because few teachers are experienced or fully prepared; and an erosion of professional development for other teachers in the building, as the basic training needed for untrained novices must be repeated year after year, impeding progress on other pedagogical needs. In addition, the researchers found these conditions create disincentives for keeping other credentialed teachers in the school. These teachers describe their embarrassment about the "lack of professionalism" and low levels of skills displayed by many uncredentialed teachers and the resulting instructional burden they experience to make up for the shortcomings of their colleagues (Shields et al., 1999, pp. 47–48).

Schools with high turnover often staff classrooms with a continuous string of short- and long-term substitute teachers (Shields et al., 1999, p. 48). This contributes to the instability students experience and to the low quality of instruction because substitutes frequently also have little preparation for teaching and there is little curricular coherence when personnel are constantly changing. Students in these heavily impacted schools experience a number of negative consequences in addition to the frequent lack of knowledge and skills on the part of individual teachers. First, students are more likely to encounter a string of such teachers, thus experiencing a cumulative effect that is more damaging to their learning than 1 year of poor teaching would create (e.g., for estimates of the cumulative effects of poor teaching, see Sanders & Rivers, 1996). Second, the "collective knowledge" of a school is weakened, and the overall expertise in the school may be inadequate to support educational decision making or collegial learning.

Finally, concentrations of new teachers create a drain on a school's finances as well as on human resources. For example, the high attrition rate of new and uncertified teachers—most of whom tend to leave within a few years (Darling-Hammond, 2003)—means that schools staffed primarily by such teachers must continually allocate funds for recruitment efforts and professional support for new teachers without reaping dividends from these investments. A recent study in Texas, using several different business cost models, found that the school system expenses of recruitment, hiring, and training associated with teacher attrition are $8,000 or more for each recruit who leaves in the first few years of teaching (Texas Center for Educational Research, 2000). Instead of using funds for needed school improvements, monies are spent in a manner that produces little long-term payoff (Carroll et al., 2000; Shields et al., 2001). Therefore, stemming the tide of attrition in these schools is critical for their ability to invest in student learning.

This Study

This study examines teacher, student, and organizational factors associated with high levels of turnover in California schools using three different measures as outcomes: (a) whether teachers report their school has a serious problem with teacher turnover, (b) whether teachers report that their schools' vacancies are difficult to fill, and (c) the proportion of beginning teachers in the school. This last measure is typically associated with turnover, although it can also, in a relatively small number of instances, be influenced by large enrollment increases that require unusual levels of hiring.

The Data Set

We used data from a survey of 1,071 California teachers conducted in January 2002 by Louis Harris Associates. The teachers represent 1,018 schools located in approximately 370 different school districts in 53 of the 58 counties in the state. Telephone interviews of teachers focused on the working conditions in their respective schools, including the adequacy of textbooks and instructional materials, physical facilities, class size and schedule, professional development opportunities, and teacher turnover and hiring. The teacher sample consisted of a random, representative sample drawn from teacher lists provided by Market Data Retrieval, with oversampling of teachers residing in lower income census tracks so as to ensure an adequate number of teachers from low-income schools (Harris, 2002). The sample was then weighted to reflect the state representative proportions of teachers working in schools by level and student composition.[2] Because of the lag time in making vendor's lists available, the sample underrepresents new teachers. By the time the list is made available and the telephone surveys are conducted, last year's new teachers have become 2nd-year teachers, if they have remained in teaching. However, the sample closely represents the state's schools. For example, the proportions of minority students in the schools represented by the two random samples of all California teachers used by Louis Harris Associates to draw their sample for this study are 61% and 60%, respectively, as compared to the 61% recorded by the California Department of Education's California Basic Educational Data System (CBEDS) data about the state's schools.

In general, inexperienced teachers have higher attrition rates than experienced teachers (NCES, 1997b). However, because our dependent variables are measures of school-level teacher turnover, rather than individual attrition, the underrepresentation of less experienced teachers does not

---

[2]Harris (2002) used three samples drawn from data purchased from Market Data Retrieval (MDR): (a) Calhome: A random sample of names and home phone numbers of teachers in MDR's database for California public school teachers; (b) Caltech: A random sample of names and school phone numbers of teachers in MDR's database for California public school teachers. Samples were drawn from both lists to secure a comprehensive and representative overall sample; and (c) Calholo: A random sample of names and school numbers of teachers in MDR's database for California public school teachers residing in lower income census tracks. Earlier survey work showed that such teachers are much more likely to teach in schools serving a greater number of low-income students.

pose the problem for our analyses that it might if we were seeking to model individual attrition decisions. The sample adequately represents the schools in which more than 20% of teachers are uncredentialed (which are, by definition, schools with large numbers of inexperienced teachers) and low-income schools where inexperienced teachers are concentrated.

Louis Harris (2002) added school-level data on student demographics from three California Department of Education databases—the Academic Performance Index, Education Data Partnership, and the CBEDS.[3] We augmented the data that Louis Harris collected with additional teacher turnover and salary data from statewide data sources. First, we added the CBEDS data on school-level teacher experience levels and created a proxy for school-level turnover by calculating the percentage of 1st-year teachers in a school.[4] This process required the school-level merging of an individual teacher's school with the CBEDS database using a unique school code.

Second, we added teacher salary information from district salary scales for each school observation. Instead of average salaries, which are affected by teacher experience levels that vary across districts, we use salary schedule measures to represent teacher salaries at three different points during their career: (a) a beginning teacher salary, represented by the lowest salary offered in the district; (b) the entry salary level for most credentialed teachers in California, represented by BA+30 (bachelor's degree plus 30 credits), Step 1; and finally (c) an advanced salary level, represented by BA+60 (bachelor's degree plus 60 credits), Step 10. The first and third measures are gathered from a California Department of Education report, whereas the second measure is taken from a California Teachers Association salary report. Both of these reports present data from the J–90 salary schedule form that districts submit to the state.

We adjusted these salary measures for cost-of-living and wage differentials across the state, using the county as a unit of analysis to capture the differences across local labor markets. We used a county's average earnings per job in 1999 (California Department of Finance, 2002) to adjust each district's salary schedule. A limitation of this measure is that the adjust-

---

[3]The Academic Performance Index data can be found at http://api.cde.ca.gov/, Education Data Partnership at http://www.ed-data.k12.ca.us/, and the California Basic Educational Data System at http://www.cde.ca.gov/demographics/coord/

[4]Because California does not track teachers using a unique teacher identifier, it is impossible for the state to calculate yearly attrition rates the way many other states do. Therefore, the percentage of 1st-year teachers is used to estimate the number of new teachers that needed to be hired at a school the year before. More advantaged schools with low turnover tend to hire experienced teachers when they have relatively rare vacancies, whereas less advantaged schools with high turnover tend to have to hire beginners in larger numbers. Therefore, a large percentage of 1st-year teachers in a school is another proxy for high turnover.

ment does not take into account the mix of jobs in a local labor market: Some have more professional jobs and others have more low-skilled labor jobs. Nonetheless, it does reflect the alternative job and wage structures facing teachers who are relatively place bound, and it compensates to a substantial extent for the large cost of living differentials across the state.[5]

Table 1 highlights the salary differences across counties for our salary schedule measures. Statewide, salaries for comparably educated and experienced teachers varied by a ratio of almost 2:1 in 2000–01. The range of salaries adjusted for the level of other county wages shows nearly a 3:1 ratio for the highest and lowest paying districts across the state, relative to their local county labor markets. These salary range estimates are conservative because they include only the districts represented in our teacher sample, or 370 of the 842 districts that report salary schedule information to the state (California Department of Education, 2002). Much of this salary variation can occur within counties. In many counties, beginning teacher salaries vary by at least $5,000 (and as much as $15,000 in Alameda County), and advanced salaries vary by at least $7,000 (and as much as $27,000 in Los Angeles County). Other studies have found similar disparities in salaries within counties (Lankford et al., 2002; Pogodzinski, 2000).

Methods

After assembling the database, we created working conditions factors to represent teachers' views of the conditions in their current school and their optimism about future school conditions. We created binary variables from questions soliciting teachers' views of specific working conditions:

Whether there are enough copies of textbooks for every student to use in class.

- Whether there are enough copies of textbooks for students to take home.
- Whether students have access to computers in the classroom.
- Whether the teacher's largest class is less than 25 students.
- Whether the teacher's largest class is greater than 33 students.
- Whether the teacher reports that his or her classroom is too small for the number of students in the class.
- Whether the school uses space for instruction that was not designed as a classroom (e.g., gymnasium, auditorium, cafeteria).
- Whether the temperature in the classroom is uncomfortable.

[5]Other similar studies of California teachers have used median home prices as an adjustment (Pogodzinski, 2000), but those data were not available for many of the counties in the state.

Table 1
Range of California Salaries, 2000–01

Salary Schedule Level	Range of Regular Salaries (County, District)		Range of Adjusted Salaries Ratio to State Average (County, District)	
	From	To	From	To
Lowest	$23,194 (Lake County, Kelseyville Unified)	$45,709 (Alameda County, Pleasanton Unified)	0.502 (Santa Clara County, Alum Rock Union Elementary)	1.601 (Calaveras County, Vallecito Union Elementary)
BA+30, step 1	$27,639 (Tehama County, Reeds Creek Elementary)	$49,591 (Alameda County, Pleasanton Unified)	0.597 (Santa Clara County, Gilroy Unified)	1.601 (Calaveras County, Vallecito Union Elementary)
BA+60, step 10	$37,278 (Fresno County, Alvina Elementary)	$69,478 (Santa Clara County, Mountain View-Los Altos Union)	0.880 (Santa Clara County, Gilroy Unified)	2.205 (Riverside County, Corona-Norco Unified)

Note. BA+30 = bachelor's degree plus 30 credits; BA+60 = bachelor's degree plus 60 credits.

- Whether the classroom has too much noise for students to concentrate.
- Whether the teacher has seen evidence of cockroaches, rats, or mice during the last year.
- Whether the school bathrooms are open and clean.

We also created four-level measures of teachers' reports about the quality of textbooks and of whether the textbooks give up-to-date information.

We created a dummy variable for whether the school schedule is "year-round multitrack." Typically, in such schools a group of teachers teach and a group of students attend for several months, stop attending for 1 month or more, and then resume attendance, whereas other groups of teachers and students use the building in the "off" times. The notion of such schedules is that, by servicing several different groups of students on different schedules, they are designed to use school buildings year round, thus increasing their capacity; and, by having shorter breaks, to avoid the long summer vacation that can negatively affect the achievement of some students. Although some approaches to modified calendars have been found to have academic benefits, schools that maintain a single-track approach to the modified calendar have had more positive outcomes than those that adopt a multitrack approach, which has more often been found to have a negative effect on achievement (e.g., see Cooper, Valentine, Charlton, & Melson, 2003).

In California, most multitrack schools were created for reasons of overcrowding, not educational preference. As several studies have reported, so-called Concept 6 multitrack schools in California's urban areas with limited facilities and increasing enrollments are so overcrowded that they must run several truncated sessions throughout the year and multiple sessions each day, resulting in a significant overall reduction in instructional time for the students, reduced access to many courses and specialized programs, increased tracking with less mobility between tracks, very large class sizes, and poorer academic performance (Herman, 1987; Oakes, 2002).

Finally, from the large number of survey questions evaluating school conditions, we conducted a factor analysis that produced two major factors: the first based on teachers' ratings of their school on eight dimensions of teaching conditions and the second based on teachers' optimism about the future for the school—that is, whether teachers believe conditions will improve—over the same eight dimensions. The component variables are based on teachers' ratings of the quality of professional development, working conditions for teachers, their own job satisfaction, quality and appropriateness of required tests for students, the way the school involves parents, the textbooks and instructional materials given, the adequacy of physical facilities, and the availability of technology.

Table 2 describes the factors. The ratings factor has an alpha of 0.81, and the optimism factor has an alpha of 0.74. For both factors, teachers' rating of their working conditions has the strongest factor loading. In the ratings factor, this is followed by teachers' ratings of physical facilities, their ratings of professional development, and their own job satisfaction; all with

Table 2

School Conditions and Teacher Optimism Factors

Variable	Observations	M	SD	Factor Loading
School conditions				
The quality of professional development	998	1.981	0.849	0.607
Working conditions for teachers	998	2.017	0.862	0.752
Your own job satisfaction	998	1.661	0.716	0.604
The quality and appropriateness of tests you are required to administer	998	2.726	0.921	0.438
The way the school involves parents	998	1.906	0.876	0.579
The text books and instructional materials you are given	998	1.921	0.732	0.549
The adequacy of physical facilities in your school	998	2.282	0.909	0.619
Availability of technology (computers & other technology)	998	2.179	0.950	0.566
Teacher optimism				
The quality of professional development	1,019	0.784	0.412	0.626
Working conditions for teachers	1,025	0.658	0.475	0.675
Your own job satisfaction	1,013	0.859	0.348	0.569
The quality and appropriateness of tests you are required to administer	1,001	0.453	0.498	0.387
The way the school involves parents	1,035	0.883	0.321	0.393
The text books and instructional materials you are given	1,028	0.844	0.363	0.428
The adequacy of physical facilities in your school	1,024	0.697	0.460	0.484
Availability of technology (computers & other technology)	1,037	0.838	0.369	0.485

Note. These are the descriptive statistics for the members of the sample with no missing data for either of the dependent variables "turnover is a problem" or "vacancies are difficult to fill" outcome. For school conditions factor, the teacher ratings for the conditions in the school ranged from 1 (*excellent*) to 4 (*poor*); eigenvalue = 2.83, α = 0.811. For teacher optimism factor, responses to the question "Looking ahead to 5 years from now, are you optimistic or pessimistic that this will be better 5 years from now?" were 0 (*pessimistic*) or 1 (*optimistic*); eigenvalue = 2.13, α = 0.735.

loadings above .60. In the optimism factor, teachers' rating of their working conditions is closely followed by their ratings of the school's professional development offerings and their own job satisfaction. Therefore, these components—which include both tangible working conditions and teachers' learning opportunities—represent the major elements of the factors that reflect teachers' views about their workplaces.

We use logit regression to develop models for each of the first two outcome variables of interest—whether turnover is a problem and whether vacancies are difficult to fill, and ordinary least squares (OLS) regression for the third outcome variable—the proportion of beginning teachers in the school. For each of these equations, we estimate three models. In the first model, we enter teacher background characteristics: age, ethnicity, education level, and teaching experience (plus a squared term). In the second model, we add school demographic characteristics: the proportions of students by racial or ethnic status, the percentage qualifying for free or reduced-price lunch, the percentage of English language learners, and location (urban, rural, suburban). In the third model, we add organizational factors including enrollment, all the working condition measures described earlier, and salary levels adjusted for county wages for entering teachers (BA+30, which is the usual entry level for a credentialed teacher in California). We found that the three measures of teacher salary were highly correlated, and we selected the entry wage as the best proxy for overall salary. High-turnover schools tend to have a disproportionate number of younger teachers, and older teachers, who are at the very top of the salary scale and who tend to stay in the same school until retirement. The next section explains the results of our analyses.

Results

Descriptive Data

Table 3 gives the means and standard deviations for the variables used in the analysis. Due to the sample source, the teachers in our sample are somewhat more experienced and educated than the average teacher in California. On average, the sampled teachers have almost 16 years of teaching experience as compared to 13 years statewide (as reflected in the CBEDS data for the 2001–02 school year). Ten of these years of experience are in their current school; statewide teachers have been in the same district for 10.3 years. Approximately 38% have obtained a master's degree or higher as compared to 31% statewide. Nine percent of the sample is Latino,

Table 3

Descriptive Statistics for Analysis Variables—Weighted

Variable	Observations	M	SD	Minimum	Maximum
Outcomes					
Turnover is a very serious or somewhat serious problem in this school	1,052	.217		0	1
School had teaching positions which could not be filled for long periods of time	1,052	.222		0	1
Teacher age					
30 or younger	1,052	0.063		0	1
31–39	1,052	0.181		0	1
40–49	1,052	0.281		0	1
50 or older	1,052	0.460		0	1
Refused	1,052	0.015		0	1
Teaching experience					
Total	1,052	15.67	7.90	1	25
In current school	1,052	9.98	7.08	1	25
Teacher educational attainment					
BA	1,052	0.631		0	1
MA	1,052	0.355		0	1
PhD	1,052	0.014		0	1
Teacher race/ethnicity					
Latino	1,052	0.087		0	1
Asian	1,052	0.026		0	1
Black	1,052	0.017		0	1
School racial/ethnic composition					
Majority Latino	950	0.268		0	1
Majority Black	950	0.155		0	1
Majority Latino and Black	950	0.161		0	1
Other composition measures					
% English language learners	1,025	22.59	21.32	0	100
% Free and reduced lunch eligible	1,024	47.77	29.69	0	100
% students eligible for Calworks	1,025	15.62	14.99	0	95
Enrollment	1,026	744.75	570.58	2	4,335

Note. These are the descriptive statistics for the sample not missing either the Turnover is a Problem outcome or the Vacancy outcome. One teacher with 25 years of experience missing education was coded as having a master's degree. Two teachers missing race/ethnicity were coded as White.

3% Asian American, and 2% Black. Across the state, 13.5% of teachers are Latino, 5.1% are African American, and 4.4% are Asian.

Twenty-two percent of teachers surveyed believe that turnover is a very serious or somewhat serious problem in their schools, and 22% also reported that their school has had teaching positions that were difficult to fill. Although there is some overlap, these measures are not the same: 10% of those who noted that turnover was not a problem said that filling vacancies was. Forty-five percent of those who said turnover was a problem reported that filling vacancies was not. This difference may reflect, in part, the extent to which schools are selective about whom they hire. Schools that insist on filling positions with highly skilled teachers may have more difficulty filling vacancies than schools with high turnover that hire whomever they can find.

The teachers in our sample taught in schools with an average enrollment of 745 students, 23% of whom were English language learners and 48% of whom qualified for free or reduced-price lunch. Seventy-five percent of teachers in the sample were teaching in urban schools. Table 4 provides the mean for teacher-reported school characteristics by the racial or ethnic composition of the students. As expected, schools differ in the racial or ethnic composition of their students. In the weighted sample, 26% of teachers reported that they teach in schools in which the majority of students are Latino. Another 16% reported that their schools have a majority of Black students, and an additional 16% reported that over 50% of students are either Black or Latino with neither group a majority. Teachers in schools with a higher proportion of Black or Latino students are more likely to be in urban areas. They are also more likely to be in multitrack schools.

There appears to be no relation between student body composition and average class size; however, there is variation in the size of the largest classes taught, which is linked to student characteristics. Sixty-seven percent of teachers teach no classes with 25 or more students, whereas 25% teach classes with 25 to 33 students; 8% teach classes with more than 33 students. Very large classes are most frequently found in schools serving a majority of Black or Black and Latino students, although the differences are not statistically significant.

Adjusted teacher salaries are higher in schools with fewer Black or Latino students. In addition, classrooms in schools with more Black or Latino students have more facilities-related problems such as uncomfortable classroom temperatures; unclean bathrooms; and evidence of cockroaches, rats, or mice. There are no evident differences by student composition in whether there are enough copies of textbooks for students (89% of the total sample), whether there are enough texts for students to take home (64%),

Table 4

School Characteristics by Student Racial/Ethnic Composition of Schools

School Characteristics	Overall	Majority Black	Majority Latino	Majority Black or Latino	Other	Missing
n	1,052	179	339	186	246	102
Urban***	0.730	0.772	0.836	0.793	0.706	0.75
Suburban***	0.167	0.161	0.125	0.168	0.168	0.21
Rural***	0.103	0.067	0.040	0.039	0.126	0.05
Multitracked***	0.142	0.109	0.279	0.126	0.153	0.18
Largest class less than 25 students	0.576	0.608	0.593	0.623	0.558	0.68
Largest class 25–33 students	0.284	0.214	0.281	0.212	0.318	0.25
Largest class greater than 33 students	0.139	0.178	0.126	0.165	0.124	0.08
Adjusted salaries BA+30**	1.095	1.034	1.102	1.061	1.117	1.07
Adjusted salaries BA+60*	1.581	1.511	1.622	1.534	1.609	1.56
Teacher rating of school conditions—factor	0.038	0.257	−0.179	−0.216	0.048	0.13
Teacher optimism about conditions improving—factor**	0.028	0.073	−0.042	−0.129	0.053	0.00
Enough copies of textbooks for every student	0.883	0.912	0.905	0.783	0.899	0.93
Enough texts for students to take home	0.640	0.615	0.624	0.571	0.662	0.69
Text condition[a],[†]	1.56	1.362	1.585	1.688	1.574	1.51
Texts are up-to-date[a],[†]	1.75	1.661	1.729	1.965	1.724	1.69
Access to computers in classroom	0.816	0.846	0.781	0.775	0.819	0.82
The classroom is too small	0.350	0.353	0.360	0.305	0.361	0.29
School uses nonclassroom space for instruction	0.315	0.330	0.314	0.303	0.314	0.41
Classroom temperature too cold or too hot[†]	0.325	0.317	0.350	0.416	0.305	0.45
Classroom too noisy***	0.215	0.165	0.261	0.263	0.214	0.25
Bathrooms are clean and open[†]	0.836	0.833	0.793	0.827	0.839	0.89
Evidence of cockroaches, rats, or mice***	0.270	0.249	0.361	0.283	0.271	0.28

Note. Means reported by groups. Chi-square test for differences across groups (unweighted tests). BA+30 = bachelor's degree plus 30 credits; BA+60 = bachelor's degree plus 60 credits.
[a]Range is 1 (*excellent*) to 4 (*poor*).
*p < .05. **p < .01. ***p < .001. [†]p < .10.

whether the classrooms are too small (36%), whether they have access to computers (78%), or whether nonclassroom space is used for classes (33% of the sample). There are no differences by student composition in the faculty rating of the school, although teachers in majority non-Black and non-Latino schools and those in majority Black schools tend to be more optimistic than those in majority Latino or majority Black and Latino schools.

Regression Analyses

In assessing the relation between turnover and school characteristics, we conducted regressions for each of the three dependent variables: whether turnover is a serious problem, whether vacancies are hard to fill, and the proportion of 1st-year teachers. In each case, we displayed three models. The first model included only teacher characteristics. The second model added demographic characteristics of the school: the racial or ethnic composition of the student body, percentage of students eligible for free or reduced-price lunch, percentage of English language learners, and whether the school is in an urban or rural area (in comparison to suburban). The third model added school factors that characterize teaching conditions, including teachers' reports of their working conditions and salaries for 1st-year teachers holding a bachelor's degree plus 30 credits (the standard entry rate for most new teachers in California).

For the first set of regressions, reported in Table 5, the outcome is whether teachers report that turnover is a problem for the school. The table gives the odds ratios and the z statistics for the estimates. Although teachers' ages and educations are not related to the probability of turnover being a problem, Black teachers are six times more likely to report a turnover problem in their school. This may be because Black teachers are more likely to be teaching in inner city schools.

In Model 2, although there is no difference in perceived turnover problems by urbanicity, we see substantially higher reported turnover problems in schools with higher proportions of Black, Latino or low-income students, as other studies have also found. The inclusion of racial composition increases the pseudo R^2 from 0.034 to 0.145.

Adding the variables included in Model 3, we find that a number of the measures of school characteristics predict turnover problems and substantially increase the predictive power of the model: The pseudo R^2 increases from 0.145 to 0.294. (In the linear probability model, the adjusted R^2 increases from 0.129 to 0.255.) Schools with lower salaries are more likely to have reported turnover problems, as are larger schools and those with multitrack schedules, lower ratings of school conditions by teachers, and

Table 5

Logit Results, Turnover Is a Serious Problem

Variables	Model 1 Odds Ratio	z Stat	Model 2 Odds Ratio	z Stat	Model 3 Odds Ratio	z Stat
Ages ≤ 30	1.494	0.85	1.748	1.37	1.751	0.92
Ages 31–40	1.312	0.89	1.542	1.54	1.274	0.68
Ages 41–50	1.161	0.58	1.239	0.92	1.087	0.30
Age missing	3.749*	2.01	4.128*	2.44	2.497	1.33
Latino	1.440	1.19	0.792	0.82	0.743	0.64
Black	6.163***	3.34	3.446*	2.16	2.485	1.56
Asian	1.765	1.13	1.080	0.16	1.009	0.02
Education—BA	0.992	0.04	1.017	0.10	1.161	0.67
Education—PhD	4.042	1.63	4.885**	2.65	1.623	0.72
Teaching experience	0.909	1.64	0.903†	1.85	0.890	1.48
Experience squared	1.003	1.50	1.003†	1.92	1.004	1.47
Majority Black			2.640***	3.65	2.626**	2.84
Majority Latino			2.073**	2.77	1.713	1.61
Majority Black or Latino			3.173***	4.55	2.891**	3.07
% Free/Reduced price lunch			1.017***	4.00	1.021***	3.51
% English learners			1.009	1.55	1.002	0.30
Urban			0.971	0.12	0.729	1.02
Rural			0.626	1.21	0.876	0.22
Enrollment					1.001*	1.97
Adjusted salaries BA+30					0.250†	1.80
Multitrack school					1.705*	1.99
School conditions factor					0.533***	4.30
Optimism factor					0.932	0.41
Evidence of rats					1.107	0.43
Enough texts					1.165	0.42
Enough texts for home					0.663	1.45
Texts in poor condition					1.212	0.89
Texts out-of-date					0.868	0.64
Computer access					0.728	1.19
Biggest class < 25 students					0.741	1.10
Biggest class > 33 students					2.469*	2.11
Classroom too small					0.842	0.76
Use nonclassroom space					1.268	1.05
Temperature problems					0.685	1.57
Classroom too noisy					1.313	1.10
Bathrooms clean and open					0.655	1.63
Linear adjusted R^2	0.0306		0.1291		0.2551	
Pseudo R^2	0.0339		0.1448		0.2937	

Note. $M = .238$, $N = 1,052$. BA+30 = bachelor's degree plus 30 credits.
*$p < .05$. **$p < .01$. ***$p < .001$. †$p < .10$.

large classes. The strongest predictor of turnover problems is teachers' rating of school conditions, which accounts for as much of the variance as the proportion of low-income students. When these school conditions variables are added, the effects of student demographics are somewhat muted; having a majority of Latino students is no longer a significant predictor of turnover problems.

We ran similar models using "difficulty filling vacancies" as the outcome. The results are given in Table 6. Here again, teacher characteristics have little influence on the outcome, whereas school student composition has a stronger effect. Teachers who report that their schools serve a majority of Black or Latino students also report more difficulty filling vacancies, as do those whose schools serve a greater percentage of English language learners. However, the predictive power of the model with student composition alone is even lower than in the turnover estimates. The pseudo R^2 increases from 0.038 in Model 1 to 0.071 in Model 2. Again, the inclusion of school characteristics in Model 3 dramatically improves the estimates (pseudo R^2 = 0.282). In this case, the estimated relation between the difficulty of filling vacancies and student body composition is reduced substantially with the inclusion of school characteristics. When school and teaching conditions are added to the model, none of the student characteristics are significant predictors of the ease or difficulty of filling vacancies. With this model, we find that larger schools, those with lower salaries, those that use multitrack schedules, those with lower ratings of school conditions, those with bigger classes, those that use nonclassroom space for classes, and those with noisy classrooms are more likely to have difficulty filling vacancies.

One concern with the first two analyses is that the teachers report both the school conditions and the outcomes. Some teachers may give all negative responses and others all positive responses. In this case, even if there were no differences in these measures across schools, we would see a correlation between outcomes and school characteristics in the data. To address this, we looked for a third outcome measure that is not teacher reported. Although it would be ideal to have turnover rates by school, we were not able to obtain this information because California does not collect such data. Instead, we used the percentage of new teachers in the school because schools with higher proportions of new teachers are hiring at high rates and typically have higher turnover rates. This variable can also be influenced by substantial year-to-year growth in school size, which may be a factor in a small number of cases that do not have high turnover.

Table 7 gives the results of similar estimations to those in Tables 5 and 6, using OLS regression to predict the percentage of 1st-year teachers in a school. For the small number of schools with multiple teachers in the sam-

Table 6
Logit Results, Vacancies Are Difficult to Fill

Variables	Model 1 Odds Ratio	z Stat	Model 2 Odds Ratio	z Stat	Model 3 Odds Ratio	z Stat
Ages ≤ 30	2.877*	2.16	2.995**	2.86	3.643*	2.20
Ages 31–40	1.180	0.45	1.267	0.88	1.063	0.16
Age 41–50	1.600†	1.74	1.708*	2.48	1.937*	2.11
Age missing	0.241	1.35	0.206	1.26	0.274	0.98
Latino	1.064*	0.19	0.815	0.74	0.715	0.79
Black	4.082	2.53	3.010*	2.12	2.291	1.41
Asian	1.598	0.87	1.159	0.32	0.962	0.08
Education—BA	0.678†	1.85	0.671*	2.43	0.667	1.62
Education—PhD	3.796	1.55	3.466*	2.19	1.366	0.43
Teaching experience	1.027	0.39	1.027	0.52	1.028	0.34
Experience squared	0.999	0.54	0.999	0.64	0.999	0.56
Majority Black			1.311	1.10	1.039	0.11
Majority Latino			1.405	1.38	0.823	0.58
Majority Black or Latino			2.190***	3.37	1.407	0.97
% Free/Reduced price lunch			1.001	0.36	1.004	0.57
% English learners			1.013*	2.19	1.007	0.92
Urban			1.123	0.51	0.880	0.33
Rural			1.482	1.21	2.556†	1.70
Enrollment					1.001**	2.96
Adjusted salaries BA+30					0.168*	2.19
Multitrack school					1.685†	1.75
School conditions factor					0.540***	3.62
Optimism factor					0.911	0.60
Evidence of rats					1.318	1.14
Enough texts					1.125	0.32
Enough texts for home					0.700	1.32
Texts in poor condition					1.402	1.64
Texts out-of-date					1.011	0.05
Computer access					1.479	1.39
Biggest class < 25 students					0.667	1.50
Biggest class > 33 students					2.223*	1.96
Classroom too small					1.334	1.17
Use nonclassroom space					1.708*	2.15
Temperature problems					1.278	1.04
Classroom too noisy					1.365	1.21
Bathrooms clean and open					0.601*	2.02
Linear adjusted R^2	0.0429		0.0548		0.2872	
Pseudo R^2	0.0383		0.0707		0.2818	

Note. $M = .208$, $N = 1,052$. BA+30 = bachelor's degree plus 30 credits.
*$p < .05$. **$p < .01$. ***$p < .001$. †$p < .10$.

Table 7

Regression Results, Percentage of First-Year Teachers

Variables	Model 1 Coeff	Model 1 t Stat	Model 2 Coeff	Model 2 t Stat	Model 3 Coeff	Model 3 t Stat
Ages ≤ 30	0.0109	0.81	0.015	1.14	0.0117	0.92
Ages 31–40	0.0015	0.17	0.004	0.45	0.0074	0.86
Ages 41–50	−0.0034	0.46	−0.001	0.14	−0.0001	0.01
Age missing	0.0201	0.86	0.026	1.05	0.0387	1.27
Latino	0.0195	1.58	0.007	0.62	0.0053	0.46
Black	0.0977***	3.30	0.083*	2.43	0.0719**	2.86
Asian	0.0303†	1.67	0.012	0.67	0.0011	0.07
Education—BA	−0.0078	1.36	−0.007	1.34	−0.0048	0.89
Education—PhD	0.0583	1.62	0.054†	1.76	0.0371	1.23
Teaching experience	−0.0041*	2.11	−0.004*	2.30	−0.0049*	2.58
Experience squared	0.0001†	1.76	0.000*	2.06	0.0001*	2.32
Majority Black			0.011	1.34	0.0062	0.77
Majority Latino			−0.008	1.01	−0.0101	1.33
Majority Black or Latino			−0.003	0.39	−0.0125	1.64
% Free/Reduced price lunch			0.00024	1.64	0.0004**	2.74
% English learners			0.00059**	2.79	0.0004*	1.98
Urban			0.013*	2.26	0.0024	0.36
Rural			0.012	0.96	0.0123	0.97
Enrollment					0.0000	1.01
Adjusted salaries BA+30					−0.0653***	3.78
Multitrack school					−0.0200**	2.92
School conditions factor					−0.0089*	2.41
Optimism factor					−0.0019	0.46
Evidence of rats					0.0023	0.37
Enough texts					−0.0140	1.40
Enough texts for home					0.0029	0.50
Texts in poor condition					0.0051	1.13
Texts out-of-date					−0.0056	1.12
Computer access					0.0060	0.79
Biggest class < 25 students					0.0071	1.16
Biggest class >33 students					0.0136	1.37
Classroom too small					−0.0011	0.17
Use nonclassroom space					0.0108†	1.85
Temperature problems					0.0076	1.33
Classroom too noisy					−0.0116†	1.87
Bathrooms clean and open					0.0111	1.52
Adjusted R^2	0.0846		0.1541		0.2346	

Note. School level, $M = .074$, $SD = .071$, $N = 827$. BA+30 = bachelor's degree plus 30 credits.

ple, we used the average of the independent variables across teachers in the school. Therefore, the regressions are run at the school level. This assures that schools with multiple respondents are not overrepresented. Table 7 shows that Black teachers and those with less experience are more likely to be in schools with a high fraction of 1st-year teachers. Schools with a higher proportion of English language learners also, on average, have more new teachers. We find no difference in percentage of 1st-year teachers among other categories of schools with different racial, ethnic, or poverty compositions. The inclusion of student composition adds some predictive power to the estimates, increasing the adjusted R^2 from 0.085 in Model 1 to 0.154 in Model 2.

Once again, school conditions, added in Model 3, are the strongest predictors of the percentage of 1st-year teachers in the school. In particular, salaries have a strong influence on the proportion of beginning teachers. In addition, whether the school is multitracked, the teachers' rating of school conditions, the use of nonclassroom space for classes, and classrooms that are too noisy all predict a greater proportion of 1st-year teachers in a school. The inclusion of these measures increases the portion of the variation explained to 23.5%.

Discussion

Using a different approach from studies that examine individual teacher attrition decisions, this study examines the predictors of high rates of school-level turnover, which are the product of many individuals' decisions and are likely related to school conditions. We find that the racial, ethnic, poverty, and language composition of a school's student body influences a school's turnover, along with its difficulty filling vacancies and proportions of beginning teachers. However, we also find that working conditions add substantial predictive power to models of turnover and that, when these working conditions are added, the influence of student demographics on reported turnover and hiring problems is reduced.

Among the strongest predictors of these outcomes is a factor representing teacher ratings of their school conditions including on one hand tangible supports for teaching in the form of teachers' working conditions, physical facilities, and availability of textbooks and technology and on the other hand the kinds of conditions that impact on the substantive aspects of teaching including the quality of professional development, the involvement of parents, and the quality and appropriateness of tests teachers are required to administer (the most negatively rated variable by the overall sample of California teachers). Another strong predictor is whether the school runs a multitrack schedule, a variable that suggests less than optimal conditions for teaching as it reflects overcrowding, very condensed daily teaching schedules that may start very early or go very late in the day, and often year-round teaching schedules that require teachers to pack up and unpack their rooms periodically throughout the school year. Although multitrack schools are more likely to have reported turnover and hiring problems, we found that they have smaller proportions of 1st-year teachers.

In estimates of turnover and difficulty filling vacancies, the presence of very large classes (33 students or more) significantly influences indicators of turnover. This result is similar to Theobald's (1990) findings regarding class size as a correlate of teacher attrition in Washington State. Other predictors include inadequate classroom space (variously captured by classes held in nonclassroom space and classrooms that are too small, too noisy, or have temperature problems) and inadequate bathrooms.

Beginning salary levels for teachers holding a BA+30 credits, adjusted for county wages, are a significant predictor of all three outcome measures. In other estimates, we also found significant relations for salaries at the BA+60 level for teachers with 10 years of experience. However, the two salary variables are collinear, so we cannot separate their effects. We include only the base salary measure in the models. The point estimates suggest that an increase in relative salaries from one to two times the local wage decreases reported turnover and vacancy problems by at least 75% and reduces the percentage of new teachers by 6.5 percentage points.

As we noted earlier, our sample underrepresents beginning teachers but closely represents school types in California. To the extent that very inexperienced teachers perceive school conditions and turnover problems differently than more experienced teachers, our estimates may not be generalizable. However, these differences in perception are unlikely to be great. Other evidence suggests that, if anything, beginning teachers are more likely than veterans to experience poor working conditions, both because they are more likely to be hired into disadvantaged schools and because they are more likely to experience the least desirable conditions within their schools (e.g., see NCTAF, 1996, 2003).

Some of the indicators of poor teaching conditions that prove important in this study—factors such as very large class sizes and multitracking—may be specific to the most underresourced schools in California, which appear to be in even more difficult straits than schools in many other states. By the late 1990s, after the decline in spending that followed the passage of Proposition 13 in 1979, California employed a greater number of underqualified teachers[6] than any other state in the country, and it ranked in the bottom decile among states on class sizes, staff:pupil ratios, libraries, and most other school resources (EdSource, 2001). In 2001, California's per pupil education spending, adjusted for cost of living, ranked 48th in the nation; reaching only 79% of the national average ($5,603 as compared to a national average of $7,079). Fully 98% of California's students were in districts that spent below the national average (Quality Counts, 2002, p. 87). Inequalities in funding have also grown. The California Postsecondary Education Commission (1998) noted

> The gap in expenditures for education between the high-spending and low-spending school districts in our state … has risen to $4,480 … . Perhaps the most disturbing part of this statewide picture is that many of the disparities noted above are consistently and pervasively related to the socioeconomic and racial–ethnic composition of the student bodies in school as well as the geographical location of schools. That is, schools in our low socioeconomic communities as well as our neighborhoods with a predominance of Black and Latino families often have dilapidated facilities, few or inadequate science laboratories, teachers in secondary schools providing instruction in classes for which they have no credential, curriculum that is unimaginative and boring, and teachers who change schools yearly and lack the professional development to complement their teaching with new instructional strategies and materials … . (p. 29)

It appears from our analysis that these kinds of conditions may contribute to high rates of turnover in the most heavily impacted schools, as well as to difficulties filling vacancies and a resulting staff mix that includes a high proportion of beginning teachers, all of which can affect the quality of education students receive.[7] This study presents evidence that reducing teacher attrition in schools where turnover is a problem may require improvements in both salaries and working conditions and that these improvements have the potential to overcome differences in schools' abilities to hire and retain teachers that have been associated with their students' characteristics.

[6]*Underqualified* is defined as teachers who lack a preliminary or clear credential in their teaching field, the standard credential recognized by California as reflecting attainment of its standards for teachers.
[7]For evidence on the negative relation between teacher inexperience and student achievement, see Betts, Rueben, and Danenberg (2000); Goe (2002); and Kain and Singleton (1996).

References

Baugh, W. H., & Stone, J. A. (1982). Mobility and wage equilibration in the educator labor market. *Economics of Education Review, 2,* 253–274.

Betts, J. R., Rueben, K. S., & Danenberg, A. (2000, February). *Equal resources, equal outcomes? The distribution of school resources and student achievement in California.* San Francisco: Public Policy Institute of California.

Boe, E. E., Bobbitt, S. A., Cook, L. H., Whitener, S. D., & Weber, A. L. (1997). Why didst thou go? Predictors of retention, transfer, and attrition of special and general education teachers from a national perspective. *The Journal of Special Education, 30,* 390–411.

Boyd, D., Lankford, L., Loeb, S., & Wyckoff, J. (in press). Explaining the short careers of high-achieving teachers in schools with low-performing students. *American Economic Review.*

Brewer, D. J. (1996). Career paths and quit decisions: Evidence from teaching. *Journal of Labor Economics, 14,* 313–339.

California Department of Education. (2002). *Selected certificated salaries and related statistics, 2000–01.* Sacramento, CA: School Fiscal Service Division.

California Department of Finance. (2002). *California county profiles: A companion to the 2001 California Statistical Abstract.* Sacramento, CA: Economic Research Division.

California Postsecondary Education Commission. (1998, December). *Toward a greater understanding of the state's educational equity policies, programs, and practices* (Commission Report 98-5). Sacramento, CA: Author.

Carroll, S., Reichardt, R., & Guarino, C. (2000). *The distribution of teachers among California's school districts and schools.* Santa Monica, CA: Rand Corporation.

Cooper, H., Valentine, J. C., Charlton, K., & Melson, A. (2003). The effects of modified school calendars on student achievement and school community attitudes: A research synthesis. *Review of Educational Research, 73,* 1–52.

Darling-Hammond, L. (1997). *Doing what matters most: Investing in quality teaching.* New York: National Commission on Teaching and America's Future.

Darling-Hammond, L. (2003). Access to quality teaching: An analysis of inequality in California's public schools. *Santa Clara University Law Review, 43,* 101–239.

EdSource. (2001, October). *How California ranks: A comparison of education expenditures.* Palo Alto, CA: Author.

Goe, L. (2002). Legislating equity: The distribution of emergency permit teachers in California. *Education Policy Analysis Archives, 10*(42). Retrieved November 8, 2002, from http://epaa.asu.edu/epaa/v10n42

Gritz, R. M., & Theobald, N. D. (1996). The effects of school district spending priorities on length of stay in teaching. *Journal of Human Resources, 31,* 477–512.

Hanushek, E. A., Kain, J. F., & Rivkin, S. G. (1999, April). *Do higher salaries buy better teachers?* (Working Paper No. 7082). Cambridge, MA: National Bureau of Economic Research.

Hanushek, E. A., Kain, J. F., & Rivkin, S. G. (2004). Why public schools lose teachers. *Journal of Human Resources, 39,* 326–354.

Harris, L. (2002). *Survey of California teachers.* Rochester, NY: Harris Interactive.

Herman, J. L. (1987). *Los Angeles experience: Evaluating the results of Concept 6.* Los Angeles, CA: UCLA Center for the Study of Evaluation.

Heyns, B. (1988). Educational defectors: A first look at teacher attrition in the NLS–72. *Educational Researcher, 17,* 24–32.

Ingersoll, R. (2001). Teacher turnover and teacher shortages: An organizational analysis. *American Education Research Journal, 38*, 499–534.

Kain, J. F., & Singleton, K. (1996, May/June). Equality of educational opportunity revisited. *New England Economic Review,* pp. 87–111.

Lankford, H., Loeb, S., & Wyckoff, J. (2002). Teacher sorting and the plight of urban schools: A descriptive analysis. *Educational Evaluation and Policy Analysis, 24,* 37–62.

Mont, D., & Rees, D. I. (1996). The influence of classroom characteristics on high school teacher turnover. *Economic Inquiry, 34,* 152–167.

Murnane, R. J., & Olsen, R. J. (1990). The effects of salaries and opportunity costs on length of stay in teaching: Evidence from North Carolina. *The Journal of Human Resources, 25,* 106–124.

Murnane, R. J., Singer, J. D., & Willett, J. B. (1989). The influences of salaries and opportunity costs on teachers' career choices: Evidence from North Carolina. *Harvard Educational Review, 59,* 325–346.

National Center for Education Statistics. (1997a). *America's teachers: Profile of a profession, 1993–94.* Washington, DC: U.S. Department of Education.

National Center for Education Statistics. (1997b). *Characteristics of stayers, movers, and leavers: Results from the Teacher Followup Survey: 1994–95.* Washington, DC: U.S. Department of Education.

National Commission on Teaching and America's Future. (1996). *What matters most: Teaching for America's future.* New York: Author.

National Commission on Teaching and America's Future. (2003). *No dream denied: A pledge to America's children.* Washington, DC: Author.

Oakes, J. (2002). *Concept 6 and busing to relieve overcrowding: Structural inequality in California schools* (Working Paper No. wws–rr012–1002). Los Angeles, CA: UCLA's Institute for Democracy, Education, & Access.

Pogodzinski, J. M. (2000). *The teacher shortage: Causes and recommendations for change.* San Jose, CA: San Jose State University, Department of Economics.

Quality Counts. (2002). *State of the states: Resources. Education week.* Washington, DC: Editorial Projects in Education.

Sanders, W. L., & Rivers, J. C. (1996). *Cumulative and residual effects of teachers on future student academic achievement.* Knoxville: University of Tennessee Value-Added Research and Assessment Center.

Scafidi, B., Sjoquist, D., & Stinebrickner, T. (2002). *The impact of wages and school characteristics on teacher mobility and retention.* Unpublished manuscript.

Shen, J. (1997). Teacher retention and attrition in public schools: Evidence from SASS '91. *Journal of Educational Research, 91,* 81–88.

Shields, P. M., Esch, C., Humphrey, D. C., Young, V. M., Gaston, M., & Hunt, H. (1999). *The status of the teaching profession: Research findings and policy recommendations. A report to the Teaching and California's Future Task Force.* Santa Cruz, CA: The Center for the Future of Teaching and Learning.

Shields, P. M., Humphrey, D. C., Wechsler, M. E., Riel, L. M., Tiffany-Morales, J., Woodworth, K., et al. (2001). *The status of the teaching profession 2001.* Santa Cruz, CA: The Center for the Future of Teaching and Learning.

Stinebrickner, T. R. (1998). An empirical investigation of teacher attrition. *Economics of Education Review, 17,* 127–136.

Texas Center for Educational Research. (2000). *The cost of teacher turnover.* Austin: Texas State Board for Teacher Certification.

Theobald, N. D. (1990). An examination of the influences of personal, professional, and school district characteristics on public school teacher retention. *Economics of Education Review, 9,* 241–250.

Theobald, N. D., & Gritz, R. M. (1996). The effects of school district spending priorities on the exit paths of beginning teachers leaving the district. *Economics of Education Review, 15,* 11–22.

Weiss, E. M. (1999). Perceived workplace conditions and first-year teachers' morale, career choice commitment, and planned retention: A secondary analysis. *Teaching and Teacher Education, 15,* 861–879.

Understanding the Relationship Between Student Achievement and the Quality of Educational Facilities: Evidence From Wyoming

Lawrence O. Picus
Rossier School of Education
University of Southern California

Scott F. Marion
The National Center for the Improvement of Educational Assessment, Inc.
Dover, New Hampshire

Naomi Calvo
Kennedy School of Government
Harvard University

William J. Glenn
Rossier School of Education
University of Southern California

A growing issue in school finance adequacy relates to the condition of school facilities and the role that the condition of those facilities plays in student learning. Using the results of standardized test scores from Wyoming students and a detailed assessment of every school building in the state of Wyoming, it can be concluded that there is essentially no relationship between the

Request for reprints should be sent to Lawrence O. Picus, USC Rossier School of Education, EDPA WPH 904C, Los Angeles, CA 90089–0031. E-mail: lpicus@usc.edu

quality of school facilities and student performance when other factors known to impact student performance are accounted for. This does not suggest investments in school facilities are not important—all children are entitled to attend school in safe, clean, and appropriate educational environments. However, policymakers should be aware that investments in facilities by themselves are unlikely to improve student learning.

During the early 1990s, many school districts responded to large influxes of new revenue from school finance reforms by spending substantial sums of money on the improvement of school facilities (Adams, 1994; Firestone, Goertz, Nagle, & Smelkinson, 1994; Picus, 1994). This behavior is consistent with the belief of most educators that the quality of school facilities has an impact on how well students do in class. Jonathan Kozol (1991) described in graphic terms the differences in the quality of school facilities among school districts in his book *Savage Inequalities*; whereas Joe Fernandez (1993) described the importance of clean, well-kept school facilities in his book *Tales Out of School*.

Very little empirical evidence supports this common belief that high-quality school facilities are a positive factor in student achievement. The lack of evidence results, in part, from the relatively poor knowledge we have about the condition of school facilities across the United States and within each state. Moreover, states that have reasonably good data on school facilities often lack sophisticated student testing systems that could be used to estimate the effect of school facilities on student performance.

One state that has good data on facilities, student performance, and student characteristics is Wyoming. Three years ago the state implemented the Wyoming Comprehensive Assessment System (WyCAS), which tests students in the 4th, 8th, and 11th grades on reading, writing, and mathematics. In addition, as part of the development of Wyoming's current school funding system, the state created a database with standardized information on the condition of every school building in the state. When combined with the student and district databases also available in Wyoming, it is possible to estimate the effect of school facilities on student performance while adequately controlling for student factors such as socioeconomic status (SES) and ethnic background as well as to control for individual school and school district circumstances. Because Wyoming is the first state with a measure of school facility quality that is reasonably consistent across school sites and districts, we now can empirically estimate the role school facilities play in student achievement, thereby making a contribution to the school finance literature on equity and adequacy.

To date, most school finance equity efforts have focused on current school district expenditures, leaving districts to fend for themselves to raise money for school construction (see Crampton, Thompson, & Hagey, 2001). If high-quality facilities play a role in student achievement, then even in highly equalized school funding systems, disparities in the quality of school buildings will still leave some children at a disadvantage. Predictably, districts with greater property wealth can finance higher quality facilities with lower tax rates, thereby placing their students in an advantageous position. Because of this possibility, states have begun to look at equalizing funding for facility construction, often a complex and expensive undertaking. Understanding the impact of facilities on student learning will help policymakers determine the cost effectiveness of this undertaking.

Facility quality also plays an important role in the growing movement to ensure adequate levels of resources for all school children. Any analysis of adequacy, which is designed to ensure that all children receive the resources they need to perform at high levels, must include a reasonable estimate of the type of school building needed to house the education program. Wyoming used its new data on school building quality to develop its adequacy-based school funding system. In the balance of this article we discuss the literature on the relationship between facilities and student performance and consider whether such a link appears to exist in Wyoming.

Facilities and Student Performance—What We Know

Conventional wisdom suggests that a school's physical environment has an impact on student learning, but researchers have had difficulty demonstrating statistically significant relationships between the physical environment and student outcomes. Despite the fact that numerous studies have been conducted on how school buildings affect student achievement, there are no conclusive findings. Many of the studies were based on the open schools movement of the 1970s and are no longer relevant to today's schools. Most of the rest were plagued with methodological problems and, not surprisingly, produce conflicting, ambiguous results.

It is difficult to study the relationship between school building quality and student achievement. Measurement problems create the first roadblock to such an analysis. School building quality is composed of numerous factors, many of which are hard to separate and most of which are hard to measure objectively. Some studies have attempted to look at each factor separately, independently assessing how paint color, carpeted or noncarpeted floors, lighting, thermal control, acoustics, and other factors affect student learning. Other studies take one composite measure such as building age and use it as a proxy for general building condition.

Both approaches are problematic. When researchers attempt to assess each factor independently, they may run into difficulties controlling for the other factors and understanding how they relate to one another. On the other hand, using a composite variable like building age may create difficulties as well, because schools are built with different lifespans. A 40-year-old building that was initially constructed to last 35 years will likely be in significantly worse condition than a similarly aged building designed to last 100 years. Also, the deferred maintenance decisions made by school officials have a profound impact on building upkeep, further obscuring the relationship between building age and condition.

In addition to measurement difficulties, school building quality studies suffer from data-availability problems. When examining how the building environment affects student learning, ideally researchers would like to control for a host of other factors such as parents' education level, parents' occupation, percentage of the student body on free lunch, median family income, percentage of single-parent families, number of student transfers, school size, length of school day, amount of instructional time, principals' experience, how districts allocate operating funds, entry-level student achievement, school climate, motivation, class size, homework and attendance policies, teacher experience and credentials, and others. Unfortunately, these data, along with an objective measure of building quality and student achievement, are rarely all available for large-scale studies. The studies that have been completed so far control for only a tiny fraction of all these factors—they might take into account only the percentage of students on free lunch, for instance—making it impossible to draw definitive conclusions about the effects of building quality alone on student learning.

Several attempts have been made to summarize the research in this field, most recently by Earthman and Lemasters (1996). They encapsulated the findings from two previous literature reviews that together covered 232 separate studies on how buildings influence students. Their main conclusion was that "even with this large number of studies, it is difficult to determine any definite line of consistent findings" (p. 3). After cautioning of serious methodological problems and difficulties in interpreting the studies, McGuffey (1982) examined the "preponderance of the evidence" and drew two major conclusions: (a) Old, obsolete buildings have a detrimental effect on student achievement, whereas modern buildings facilitate learning, and (b) building conditions have a differing impact across grades and subjects. Specifically, McGuffey found that research indicated that school building age, thermal factors, lighting quality, color, acoustic factors, and school size are factors that significantly affect student achievement, whereas no relationship was found for open space, amount of space, windowless facilities, and underground facilities.

In a relatively early study, McGuffey and Brown (1978) examined the relationship between building age and student achievement. Using the school district as the unit of analysis, they regressed student achievement variables on the number of classrooms constructed in each decade and SES. They found that SES explained roughly 55% of the variance in 4th-grade test scores, 20% of 8th-grade scores, and 9% of 11th-grade scores. Adding the percentage of classrooms constructed in each decade explained an additional 3% of the variance at most. In some instances, the percentage of classrooms built in a particular decade had a positive relationship to student achievement, whereas in other cases it had a negative effect. Although the results did not appear to have a particular pattern and were in some cases contradictory, the authors concluded that building age has an impact on student achievement beyond SES and that it appears to have a differential impact across grade levels and subject matter. They suggested that building age has the most influence on reading and math scores and that it affects 4th- and 11th-grade students much more than 8th-grade students.

The McGuffey and Brown (1978) study is problematic for several reasons. The researchers used building age as a proxy for building condition, stating that building age is "a measure of the cumulative effects of the thermal, visual, acoustical, and aesthetic environment" (p. 7). However, the relationship between building age and building condition has not been firmly established. Moreover, that measure also obscures any potential differences of the effects of the various individual factors such as lighting, thermal conditions, maintenance, and so forth. Also, using the percentage of classrooms constructed in each decade is a problematic measure because it does not reflect the overall age spread in the district. For instance, if 30% of a district's classrooms were built in the 1950s, one might predict that the 1950s variable would have either a positive or negative effect on student achievement, depending on whether the other 70% were built in the 1920s or the 1970s. Another problem results from the choice of McGuffey and Brown to use the school district as the unit of analysis. Because building condition, student scores, and socioeconomic factors tend to vary across schools within a district, using the district as the unit of analysis is too gross of a measure to accurately assess the relationship between building condition and achievement. In addition, the authors did not control for any factors other than SES.

Other researchers have obtained contradictory results on whether building age is related to student achievement. Because it is an objective measure with readily available data, researchers would like to be able to use building age as a proxy for building condition. Although several early studies found a relationship between the two, some more recent studies have not. Building age is not necessarily a sound reflection of condition because buildings are built with different projected lifespans and receive differing amounts of maintenance.

One option researchers could consider is using the percentage of the lifespan attained rather than age itself as the independent variable, perhaps controlling for the level of maintenance funding. Another issue is that building age is not a particularly useful variable even if it does turn out to have a direct relationship to student achievement, because it would be impractical to replace schools every 10 years or so to ensure they were constantly "modern." It is more important to discover what aspects of building conditions in particular are important to student achievement and thus know what areas of maintenance (or levels of funding) are most important.

In the first of a series of more recent studies on the relationship between building condition and student achievement, Berner (1993) used a regression model to look at student achievement in Washington, DC schools. School buildings were rated as poor, fair, or excellent based on information from a parent advocacy group that had organized groups of volunteer maintenance workers, architects, engineers, and others to assess building condition. Schools' average scores on the Comprehensive Test of Basic Skills (CTBS) were used as the measure of student achievement. As expected, the two demographic variables that were included in the regression (the percentage of the neighborhood population that was White and the mean income of the school neighborhood) were found to be positively related to student achievement. School size was another significant factor: Berner found that an increase of 100 students predicted a reduction in the average achievement scores by 8.8 points. Finally, building condition was also positively related to student achievement: Increasing from one rating category to the next, test scores can be expected to increase by 5.5 points. Together, these factors explained 34% of the variance in student achievement. The other two variables included by Berner, school age and school level, were not found to be significantly related to student achievement.

Berner (1993) concluded that building condition affects student learning, although she pointed out several weaknesses of her study. First, she noted that selection bias was possible because motivated parents could have placed their children in the schools with better facilities. Second, she cautioned that omitted variable bias may significantly weaken her study because she did not include a number of factors that are believed to explain variance in student achievement. In addition to these two problems cited by Berner, there are other reasons to regard her results as tentative at best. She did not address the reliability of the rating system for building condition, making it difficult to know how robust a measure it is. Also, the ratings of building condition and the student achievement scores came from the early 1990s, but her demographic variables were from the 1980 census, which provided neighborhood demographic data rather than information regarding the school's student body. Therefore, a data mismatch existed, unless all the schools in Washington, DC had admissions policies restricted to neighborhood members. Finally, Berner did not report what percentage of the variance in student scores building condition explained, once demographic factors are considered. Keeping in mind that her entire model explained only 34% of the variance, it is probable that building condition was responsible for only a tiny fraction of it.

In a study similar to Berner's, Cash (1994) looked at building condition, student achievement, and student behavior in rural high schools in Virginia. Building condition was self-reported by school district personnel and was divided into two categories: cosmetic and structural. Cash found that higher building quality was related to higher student achievement (the difference in percentile rankings was as much as 5%). Cosmetic factors appeared to have more of an effect on student achievement than structural condition. Cash also found that higher rated schools unexpectedly had *more* disciplinary problems and was unable to explain why this might be so.

In a follow-up study, Earthman, Cash, and Van Berkum (1995) used a sample consisting of all 199 high school buildings in North Dakota. The 13 subtests of the CTBS were used as the measure of academic achievement, whereas the number of reported disciplinary incidents per pupil was the measure of behavior. The building condition data came from a survey filled out by principals. Buildings were ranked into three categories: The bottom 25% were labeled substandard, the middle 50% were considered standard, and the top 25% were above standard. Instead of computing statistical analyses on the data, the researchers presented tables displaying the means of the substandard and above-standard groups only. No mention was made of the standard group in their results.

Earthman et al. (1995) found that students in above-standard buildings outscored their counterparts in substandard buildings on most but not all of the CTBS subtests, by 1 to 9 percentile points. However, when considering structural factors alone, students in substandard buildings outscored those in above-standard buildings on the four math and social studies subtests by 3 to 12 percentile points. In addition, out of the 18 categories on the building evaluation survey, students in buildings rated substandard on 5 of the categories (building age, air conditioning, noise, exterior painting, and acreage) scored higher than those in above-standard buildings. The researchers give no explanation for this, except to comment that it is probably an anomaly. Because they failed to conduct a statistical comparison of means, it is difficult to interpret the data.

Despite these weak and ambiguous findings, the authors declared that the evidence supports a positive relationship between building condition and student achievement. However, their analysis is plagued with methodological problems in addition to the data interpretation issues just discussed. The researchers failed to conduct any statistical analyses on their data, reporting only means within two of the categories of school condition. They only examined the top and bottom 25% of the schools, leaving half of the sample out of their analysis. Their measure of building condition was self-reported by the building principal, but they made no attempt to assess the reliability of the measure or obtain an external opinion regarding building condition. The rating system also required principals to rate each item as "present" or "absent," leaving no room for a range of conditions. Also, automatically rating the bottom 25% of the buildings as substandard obscures actual building condition. Perhaps all of the schools in North Dakota are in relatively good condition, in which case even the bottom 25% might be more than adequate. Alternatively, they could all be rapidly decaying, making even the top 25% substandard. The authors did not explain how they controlled for other variables that could be expected to have an impact on student achievement. (They stated that the mean scores are adjusted for SES but do not mention how they compute this.) Finally, their evidence does not appear to support their conclusions. The authors made no attempt to explain why students in substandard buildings should outscore those in above-standard buildings on math and social studies when theory does not suggest that this should be the case. This leads to the absurd implication that to improve student achievement in most subjects, principals should make cosmetic changes in the classrooms but to improve math or social studies scores, they should let the building structurally deteriorate.

McGuffey's (1982) finding that building conditions have a differing impact across grade levels and subjects is difficult to explain, given that the underlying theory suggests that facilities affect behavior, which in turn affects learning. The theoretical base is best summarized by a 1989 Carnegie Foundation for the Advancement of Teachers report:

> The report acknowledged that a good building does not necessarily make a good school, but points out that students' attitudes toward education and the prospect of educational success are a reflection of their environment. The report notes that "the tacit message of the physical indignities in many urban schools is not lost on students." It bespeaks ne-

glect, and students' conduct seems simply an extension of the physical environment that surrounds them. (Berner, 1993, p. 9)

There is nothing in this theory to explain why some grade levels would be more affected by building condition than others. The more puzzling issue is why some subjects, like math and social studies, would be affected differently. The theory runs into further difficulty because the link between facilities and student behavior is even more tenuous than the link between facilities and achievement. For example, some of the studies that claim to find a positive relationship between building condition and student learning also report finding a negative relationship between facility quality and student behavior.

McGuffey (1982) acknowledged that facilities have a very small potential impact on student learning but argued that they are one of the few variables that affect student learning over which school officials have complete control. Given this, he claimed that schools should make every effort to ensure high-quality facilities. However, it is extremely costly to build, maintain, and renovate facilities, so it may be more cost effective to use that money elsewhere. Improved carpeting in a school may come at the expense of hiring more or better teachers because schools lack unlimited resources. Schools need to get the maximum return for the money they spend. Therefore, studies that claim facilities benefit student learning must take costs into consideration so that schools can assess whether installing air-conditioning, painting the walls certain colors, or adding better lighting will raise student scores or whether they are better off buying new textbooks. Cost–benefit analyses of the impact of facilities might be productive lines of research, but first it must be shown that facilities have a positive impact at all.

Several other studies have suggested that cosmetic building condition has a greater effect on student achievement than structural condition for which the reported effect seems to range from weak to none at all. The authors of these studies failed to discuss the implications of these findings, which appear to support routine maintenance efforts rather than the construction of new state-of-the-art schools. This approach is actually in line with the underlying theory because, although students would be expected to notice cosmetic features, they would be less likely to be affected by structural problems on a day-to-day level. This is not to say that structural factors are unimportant. Whether or not structural factors have a direct influence on student achievement, it is important to maintain buildings for safety and financial reasons.

In summary, the evidence documenting the link between facilities and student learning is weak at best. Better measures and methodologies are needed, and researchers should give some thought to developing a sounder underlying theory.

Estimating the Relationship Between Facilities and Student Performance in Wyoming

Wyoming presents a unique opportunity to more accurately study the relationship between school facilities and student performance. In response to court rulings in the *Campbell v. Wyoming*[1] case, the state has implemented an adequacy-based school funding system. In its ruling, the Wyoming Supreme Court also declared the state's capital construction funding system unconstitutional. In response, the state has conducted an assessment of every school building in the state and estimated that it will cost some $563 million to bring all of the facilities to the level required by the court. The state's assessments provide a richer dataset than any of the other researchers were able to use.

In this section of the article we describe the procedures the state used to assess the quality of school buildings. We also discuss the student performance data available in Wyoming. Finally, we describe the results of our analyses on the impact of facilities on student performance.

Method

Data sources. The data used for this study came from two primary sources: building quality scores produced by the consulting firm MGT of America, Inc. (MGT), and reading, mathematics, and writing scores from the WyCAS. MGT was contracted by the state of Wyoming to evaluate the condition, educational suitability, and technological readiness of each school facility in Wyoming. These evaluations were conducted in 1997 and 2000.

MGT calculated a single building condition score for each building based on an instrument it created and was designed to be objective. The building condition scores were determined by collectively assessing up to 22 separate building subsystems such as foundations, ceilings, floors, and so forth. The individual rating tools consisted of 1 to approximately 20 questions (depending on the particular building), the answers of which were agreed on by a school representative and the assessor (a subcontractor to MGT; usually an architect, contractor, or building supervisor). MGT

---

[1]*Campbell County School District v. State* (1995) and *State v. Campbell County School District* (2001).

weighted the subsystem assessments relative to the cost of bringing the affected components up to an "as new" condition. For example, the score for the more costly foundation–structure category was weighted more heavily than the score for ceilings or floors. The published overall condition score was the average of the weighted values of all the applicable subsystems. The state used the condition scores when it estimated the anticipated costs of bringing all school facilities up to the standard demanded by the Wyoming Supreme Court.

The suitability tool possessed a higher degree of subjectivity than the building condition instrument because it was 95% self-reported by district superintendents or their designees. The suitability tool purported to measure the degree to which each building was suitable for its current use. It included some items that could be corrected easily and others over which the school staff has no control (e.g., whether the school was designed specifically for the grades now served). Because of its greater subjectivity, the state does not appropriate capital construction dollars on the basis of this instrument. Instead, it was used to help districts with their facility planning needs.

This study relates student achievement (as discussed later) to the results of the facilities assessments. Following the Wyoming Supreme Court, this study focuses primarily on building condition scores, although we also analyzed the relationship between suitability scores and student achievement. In all cases, we used the most recent assessment score available for each building.

We estimated student achievement using the WyCAS, which is a set of tests administered to all 4th-, 8th-, and 11th-grade students in all Wyoming public schools, accredited institutions, and accredited private schools. These assessments are designed to measure student achievement relative to the Wyoming content and performance standards in reading, writing, and mathematics and comprise both multiple choice and open-ended test questions. Each student at the specific grade level answered certain common items, plus a set of matrix-sampled items that were drawn from a large pool of test questions that are distributed across eight forms of the test. Matrix sampling has the advantage of allowing schools to receive information from many more test items than would be possible if only common items were administered. It has the benefit of yielding higher levels of reliability at the school level because reliability is highly correlated with test length.[2] In addition, matrix sampling reduces the likelihood that teachers could prepare students for specific test items because they do not know

[2]For more information about the WyCAS, please visit http://www.MeasuredProgress.org/wycas/index.htm

which of the matrix-sampled items will appear on a given version of the test.

The WyCAS was used as the measure of student achievement in this investigation for several reasons. First, it is the only standards-based measure administered in all Wyoming schools that had a 4th-, 8th-, or 11th-grade class. Second, it is an exceptionally high-quality set of assessments. Finally, it provides a high-quality sample because essentially all students in the required grades participate in the WyCAS. Although it is limited to reading, writing, and mathematics, these subject areas form the core curriculum and serve as useful proxies of school learning. Performance in most academic areas is highly related, with reading being the skill area that correlates strongest with the other areas. Very few schools would excel in science or social studies, for instance, and not be successful in reading and mathematics.

Analyses. The WyCAS was first administered in 1999. We included 3 years of WyCAS results (1999–01) and involved over 60,000 Wyoming students in this study. We opted to use multiyear average scores to provide a considerably more stable estimate of a school's performance than could be obtained by relying on any single year. Two different measures of each school's achievement in each content area were used: the 3-year average of the percentage of students who scored in the proficient and advanced performance levels, and the 3-year average of the scale scores. In both cases, the averages for reading, writing, and mathematics were combined to arrive at an overall proxy of student achievement for the school. Using the percentage of students scoring at the proficient and advanced levels has the advantage of familiarity because that is the statistic most often reported in the press. On the other hand, the scale score, with a range from 200 to 280, has a continuous and normal distribution and is therefore the more appropriate measure to use in a correlational study. Further, the scale score has the advantage of taking each student's score into account, whereas the proficiency standard only uses the scores of the highest performing students. This could produce misleading results if, for example, a school with a large number of low-performing students chose to increase its percentage of proficient and above by focusing its efforts on students performing just below the proficient level.

Using multiple subject areas across multiple years has the statistical benefit of incorporating more items and effectively more students into a single proxy, thus making this proxy more reliable and stable than if a single content area for a single year was used. However, to evaluate the robustness of these analyses, correlations with building scores were computed separately for each grade level for each content area and year.

The majority of the analyses described in this study use bivariate correlational analyses with the school building as the unit of analysis. Bivariate correlations only offer a description of the direction and magnitude of the relationship between two variables and do not take into account the influence of any additional factors. This provides a good initial indication of whether two variables are related but can often lead to misleading inferences. The possibility exists that another variable could account for the relationship, or lack thereof, between building condition and WyCAS scores. Generally, there is a presence of additional explanatory variables when trying to help disentangle a stronger-than-expected relationship between two variables, not when the variables appear unrelated. To perform a more in-depth analysis of the relationship, we included a measure of SES in the analyses.

It is difficult to find valid measures of SES that can be tied to specific school buildings. However, the percentage of students receiving free or reduced lunches can serve as a useful proxy for building level SES. Unfortunately, middle and high school students tend not to take advantage of the free and reduced price lunch opportunities to the same degree as elementary school students and their parents; therefore, the percentage of free and reduced price lunch students tends to be a better SES proxy for elementary than secondary schools (Odden & Picus, 2004). Therefore, the analyses incorporating the free and reduced price lunch statistic are limited to elementary school buildings.

The effect of adding the SES proxy into the study was evaluated using multiple regression analyses. Multiple regression is a correlational statistical technique that permits the evaluation of the degree of relationship between two variables while factoring out the influence of one or more additional variables. In this case, multiple regression analyses were used to examine the relationship between building and WyCAS scores while factoring out the influence of SES.

Findings

The descriptive statistics for all of the variables used in this study are found in Appendix A. The mean building condition score for all of the schools in the study was 72.38 ($SD = 14.73$; see Appendix A, Table A4), whereas the distribution had a slight negative skew (see Appendix A, Figure 1). Two important facts are noticeable in this figure: 7.1% of the school buildings had a condition score below 50, and only 12.5% of the schools scored above 90. These are important cutoff points because the Wyoming Supreme Court stated that the condition of all schools must be improved until they reach a score of 90, with immediate attention required for all schools scoring below 50.

The suitability score scale had a mean of 71.28 (SD = 18.28), but the distribution was more negatively skewed than the distribution of condition scores (see Appendix A, Figure 2). The range of the suitability scores is wider than that of the building condition scores, which may result from the higher level of subjectivity in the suitability tool.

The 3-year WyCAS average composite scores had a mean of 234.60 (SD = 6.09). The distribution was essentially normal (see Appendix A, Figure 3), making it consistent with the assumptions of correlation analysis.

Condition Score Analyses

The correlation between the 1999–01 WyCAS average composite scale scores and the building condition scores for the full sample and for any of the grade levels is essentially zero (see Table 1). This finding results whether the independent variable is any of the single-year composite scores or any of the multiyear content area average scores. Additional analyses confirming these findings with single-year and single-subject variables are presented in Appendix B.

These findings are also replicated when the percentage of students scoring proficient or above in each of the three content areas is used in the analyses instead of scale score averages and composites (see Table 2). The correlation coefficients confirm that no relationship was found between building condition scores and multiyear and multigrade WyCAS scores. This finding implies that as building scores improve, there is no likelihood that WyCAS scores will either improve or decline.

Table 1

Pearson Correlation Coefficients Between Building Scores and Various WyCAS Average and Composite Scale Scores

Measure	All Grades[a]	4th Grade[b]	8th Grade[c]	11th Grade[d]
Reading 3-year scale score average	.00	−.01	.01	.00
Writing 3-year scale score average	.00	.02	.02	−.04
Math 3-year scale score average	.00	.01	−.01	−.04
Composite scale score 1999	.02	.02	.03	.02
Composite scale score 2000	−.01	−.02	.02	−.02
Composite scale score 2001	−.03	.01	−.05	−.07
1999–01 WyCAS composite average	−.01	.00	.00	−.03

Note. WyCAS = Wyoming Comprehensive Assessment System.
[a]n = 296. [b]n = 155. [c]n = 74. [d]n = 67.

Table 2

Pearson Correlation Coefficients Between Building Condition Scores and Percentage of Students Scoring Proficient or Advanced on the Wyoming Comprehensive Assessment System

Measure	All Grades[a]	4th Grade[b]	8th Grade[c]	11th Grade[d]
Reading 3-year % proficient & advanced	.02	−.01	.04	.02
Writing 3-year % proficient & advanced	.01	.04	.04	−.03
Math 3-year % proficient & advanced	.02	.06	−.01	−.03

[a]$n = 296$. [b]$n = 155$. [c]$n = 74$. [d]$n = 67$.

Table 3

Correlation Between Building Condition Scores and Improvement in Wyoming Comprehensive Assessment System Average Composite Scale Scores

Measure	All Grades[a]	4th Grade[b]	8th Grade[c]	11th Grade[d]
Difference between 1999–00 average composite and 2001 composite	−.06	.00	−.15i	−.11

[a]$n = 294$. [b]$n = 154$. [c]$n = 74$. [d]$n = 66$.

We also examined the relationship between improvement on WyCAS and building scores. It could be argued that higher quality buildings are related to improvement rather than status (i.e., average scores). Our findings, however (presented in Table 3), do not support this assumption. The correlation between building condition scores and improvement in WyCAS average composite scale scores is essentially zero for both the full sample and any of the individual grade levels.

The multiple regression analysis tested whether other variables could have influenced the results of the bivariate correlations. Our results indicate that even with the influence of SES statistically controlled, there was still no discernable relationship between WyCAS scores and building condition scores (see Table 4). The standardized regression coefficient (beta) uses the same 0 to ±1 scale as the simple correlations and, thus, can be interpreted in the same fashion. The results presented in Table 4 document that even with SES statistically controlled, building condition scores are totally unrelated to student achievement as measured by WyCAS. As expected, SES has a strong relationship with achievement.

In connection with this analysis, we made the interesting finding that the correlation between building condition scores and the percentage of students receiving free or reduced price lunch was essentially zero ($r = .03$). This lack of correlation means that we found no relationship between building conditions and the poverty level of the school. In other words, poorer students are not necessarily in lower quality buildings; more affluent students are not necessarily in higher quality buildings. Therefore, one could argue that equity in Wyoming has been achieved, at least in terms of school building quality.

Suitability Score Analyses

The relationship between the suitability scores and WyCAS scores is generally similar to the relationship between building condition scores and WyCAS scores (see Table 5). Additional analyses confirming these findings with single-year and single-subject variables are presented in Appendix B. However, there appears to be a small, positive relationship be-

Table 4

Multiple Regression Results With 1999–01 Wyoming Comprehensive Assessment System Composite Average as the Dependent Variable and Condition Scores and Percentage of Students Receiving Free and Reduced Price Lunch Services and Independent Variables

Measure	Unstandardized Coefficients		Standardized Coefficients		
	B	SE	B	T	p
Constant	237.61	2.32		102.47	.00
Condition score	0.00	0.03	.01	0.10	.92
% of free and reduced price lunch students	−12.99	1.64	−.53	−7.93	.00

Note. Elementary schools only, $n = 162$. $r = .53$; $r^2 = .28$; SEM = 5.08.

Table 5

Pearson Correlation Coefficients Between Suitability Scores and Various WyCAS Average and Composite Scale Scores

Measure	All Grades[a]	Grade 4[b]	Grade 8[c]	Grade 11[d]
Reading 3-year scale score average	.07	.06	−.07	.16
Writing 3-year scale score average	.10	.04	−.05	.14
Math 3-year scale score average	.08	.05	−.05	.19
Composite scale score 1999	.18*	.11	.01	.37**
Composite scale score 2000	.06	.03	−.08	.09
Composite scale score 2001	.01	−.01	−.12	.03
1999–01 WyCAS average composite	.09	.05	−.07	.19

Note. WyCAS = Wyoming Comprehensive Assessment System.
[a]$n = 292$. [b]$n = 151$. [c]$n = 73$. [d]$n = 68$.
*$p \leq .05$. **$p \leq .01$.

tween suitability and WyCAS scores at the 11th-grade level, which is statistically significant for the 1999 composite scale score. These results may show that suitability has more of an effect at the high school level where specialized equipment such as science laboratories and computer workstations are more prevalent. However, given the number of analyses conducted for this study, we should be cautious about treating this finding as anything other than a chance occurrence or an anomaly in the data.

As with the building condition analysis, we next considered the impact of suitability on the proficiency scores. When studying the percentage of students scoring in the proficient and advanced categories, the pattern is similar to the analyses using the scale scores (see Table 6). The only significant relationship we found was between suitability and writing achievement.

The relationship between improvement of WyCAS scores and suitability scores reveals a different pattern (see Table 7). The relationship was negative and significant for 11th grade as well as for the full sample. This means that higher building suitability scores are associated with lower rates of WyCAS improvement. As with the correlations reported in Tables 5 and 6, these coefficients should be viewed as indicative of very weak relationships.

Table 6

Pearson Correlation Coefficients Between Building Suitability Scores and Percentage of Students Scoring Proficient or Advanced on the Wyoming Comprehensive Assessment System

Measure	All Grades[a]	Grade 4[b]	Grade 8[c]	Grade 11[d]
Reading 3-year % proficient & advanced	.03	.07	−.07	.19
Writing 3-year % proficient & advanced	.12*	.03	−.04	.16
Math 3-year % proficient & advanced	.08	.06	−.01	.17

[a]$n = 292$. [b]$n = 151$. [c]$n = 73$. [d]$n = 68$.
*$p \leq .05$.

Table 7

Correlation Between Building Suitability Scores and Improvement in Wyoming Comprehensive Assessment System Average Composite Scale Scores

Measure	All Grades[a]	Grade 4[b]	Grade 8[c]	Grade 11[d]
Difference between 1999–00 average composite and the 2001 composite	−.17**	−.13	−.15	−.27*

[a]$n = 290$. [b]$n = 150$. [c]$n = 73$. [d]$n = 67$.
*$p \leq .05$. **$p \leq .01$.

Table 8

Multiple Regression Results With 1999–01 Wyoming Comprehensive Assessment System Composite Average as the Dependent Variable and Suitability Scores and Percentage of Students Receiving Free and Reduced Price Lunch Services and Independent Variables

Measure	Unstandardized Coefficients		Standardized Coefficients		
	B	SE	B	T	p
Constant	237.75	1.84		128.98	.00
Suitability score	0.00	0.02	.00	0.00	1.00
% of free and reduced price lunch students	−12.95	1.70	−.53	−7.62	.00

Note. Elementary schools only, $n = 162$. $R = .53$; $R^2 = .28$; $SEM = 5.15$.

The slight positive and slight negative bivariate correlation coefficients reported in Tables 5, 6, and 7 lead to some uncertainty about what would be most appropriate to infer about the relationship between a building's suitability and its WyCAS scores. The multiple regression analysis that included an SES proxy in the analyses shed some light on the relationship. With SES statistically controlled, there was no relationship between WyCAS and building suitability scores (see Table 8).

In addition, the bivariate relationship between percentage of students receiving free and reduced lunch price and building suitability scores was slightly negative (−0.11) but not statistically different than zero. The sign of the coefficient is consistent with the expected result that schools with higher percentages of students receiving free and reduced price lunch tend to be associated with relatively lower building suitability scores. However, the lack of statistical significance means that these data do not support the inference that SES is related to suitability.

Conclusions

This study was designed to examine whether higher quality buildings are related to student performance using data from Wyoming. By comparing measures of building condition and suitability to both student test scores and improvement in student test scores, we attempted to ascertain whether the condition or suitability of facilities impacts WyCAS scores or WyCAS improvement. The results of these analyses clearly indicate that there is essentially no relationship between building condition or suitability (as measured by MGT scores) and student achievement as measured by

WyCAS, meaning higher quality buildings are unrelated to higher levels of student academic achievement. The robustness of this finding is conclusively demonstrated in dozens of separate analyses using both building condition scores and building suitability scores. These findings are critically important given the recent supreme court decision in Wyoming about the need to infuse more money into the capital construction budget as well as similar decisions in other states across the nation.

This study does not dispute the need for each child to attend school in a safe school building or the importance of buildings to be able to accommodate modern technology or other similar requirements. However, improving the technological readiness of a school building is considerably less expensive than the costs of meeting the Wyoming Supreme Court's requirement that school condition be brought up to a score of 90.

Public school resources are not unlimited. When resources are spent on facilities, generally there is less available for other programs that research shows can improve student learning. The substantial literature on the importance of high-quality teachers, strong educational leaders, a rich and comprehensive curriculum, and parent involvement suggests there are other ways to invest educational resources that will have a greater potential impact on student learning.

References

Adams, J. E. (1994). Spending school reform dollars in Kentucky: Familiar patterns and new programs, but is this reform? *Educational Evaluation and Policy Analysis, 16*, 375–390.

Berner, M. M. (1993). Building conditions, parental involvement, and student achievement in the District of Columbia public school system. *Urban Education, 28*, 6–29.

Campbell County School District v. State, 907 P2d 1238 (Wyo. 1995).

Cash, C. S. (1994). *Building conditions and student achievement and behavior*. Unpublished doctoral dissertation, Virginia Polytechnic Institute and State University, Blacksburg, Virginia.

Crampton, F. E., Thompson, D. C., & Hagey, J. M. (2001). Creating and sustaining school capacity in the twenty-first century: Funding a physical environment conducive to student learning. *Journal of Education Finance, 27*, 633–652.

Earthman, G., Cash, C., & Van Berkum, D. (1995, October). *A statewide study of student achievement and behavior and school building condition*. Paper presented at the annual meeting of the Council of Educational Facility Planners, International, New York.

Earthman, G., & Lemasters, L. (1996, October). *Review of research on the relationship between school buildings, student achievement, and student behavior*. Paper presented at the annual meeting of the Council of Educational Facility Planners, International, New York.

Fernandez, J. (1993). *Tales out of school: Joseph Fernandez's crusade to save American education*. New York: Little, Brown.

Firestone, W. A., Goertz, M. E., Nagle, B., & Smelkinson, M. F. (1994). Where did the $800 million go? The first years of New Jersey's Quality Education Act. *Educational Evaluation and Policy Analysis, 16*, 359–374.

L. O. Picus et al.

Kozol, J. (1991). *Savage inequalities: Children in America's schools.* New York: Crown.
McGuffey, C. (1982). Facilities. In H. J. Walberg (Ed.), *Improving educational standards and productivity* (pp. 237–281). Berkeley, CA: McCutchan.
McGuffey, C., & Brown, C. (1978). The impact of school building age on school achievement in Georgia. *The Educational Facility Planner, 2,* 5–19.
Odden, A. R., & Picus, L. O. (2004). *School finance: A policy perspective* (3rd ed.). New York: McGraw-Hill.
Picus, L. O. (1994). The local impact of school finance reform in four Texas school districts. *Educational Evaluation and Policy Analysis, 16,* 391–404.
State v. Campbell County School District, 19 P.3d 518 (Wyo. 2001).

Appendix A
Descriptive Statistics

Table A1

Descriptive Statistics for the Variables Used in This Study: Fourth Grade

Measure	N	Minimum	Maximum	M	SD
Reading scale score 1999	156	216	250	235.88	6.31
Writing scale score 1999	156	218	248	235.09	6.11
Math scale score 1999	156	209	249	231.33	7.33
Reading scale score 2000	156	213	253	233.73	7.13
Writing scale score 2000	156	208	251	232.75	7.80
Math scale score 2000	156	206	245	227.71	7.73
Reading scale score 2001	158	218	260	236.48	7.02
Writing scale score 2001	158	220	255	236.39	6.80
Math scale score 2001	158	206	255	230.73	8.18
Reading 3-year scale score average	158	217	255	235.55	6.26
Writing 3-year scale score average	158	218	256	234.80	6.25
Math 3-year scale score average	158	208	256	230.09	7.33
Reading 3-year % prof & adv	158	9	83	49.98	13.68
Writing 3-year % prof & adv	158	10	78	36.21	13.40
Math 3-year % prof & adv	158	1	83	33.81	14.37
Building condition score	155	33.53	100	72.64	13.39
Building suitability score	151	17	99	68.80	17.62
Composite scale score 1999	156	214.45	246.52	234.10	6.13
Composite scale score 2000	156	208.86	247.15	231.39	7.00
Composite scale score 2001	158	216.33	251.67	234.53	6.92
1999–01 WyCAS average composite	158	214.67	251.33	233.45	6.07
Difference between 2001 composite score and 1999–00 average composite	155	–9.92	13.16	1.57	4.60

Note. prof & adv = proficient and advanced performance levels; WyCAS = Wyoming Comprehensive Assessment System.

Table A2

Descriptive Statistics for the Variables Used in This Study: Eighth Grade

Measure	N	Minimum	Maximum	M	SD
Reading scale score 1999	75	217	248	234.69	5.54
Writing scale score 1999	75	221	252	241.15	6.26
Math scale score 1999	75	208	242	229.61	6.56
Reading scale score 2000	76	214	243	232.54	6.39
Writing scale score 2000	76	218	250	237.11	6.48
Math scale score 2000	76	204	248	230.15	7.74
Reading scale score 2001	77	214	250	234.58	6.39
Writing scale score 2001	77	218	255	239.21	6.90
Math scale score 2001	77	205	242	230.26	7.00
Reading 3-year scale score average	77	216	245	233.83	5.80
Writing 3-year scale score average	77	218	251	239.01	6.25
Math 3-year scale score average	77	205	241	230.08	6.79
Reading 3-year % prof & adv	77	5	63	37.78	12.88
Writing 3-year % prof & adv	77	10	84	51.55	15.77
Math 3-year % prof & adv	77	0	53	30.44	12.01
Building condition score	74	32.73	100	71.96	16.62
Building suitability score	73	30	100	72.19	19.07
Composite scale score 1999	75	215.53	245.70	235.15	5.82
Composite scale score 2000	76	212.29	245.97	233.26	6.62
Composite scale score 2001	77	213.33	246.00	234.68	6.36
1999–01 WyCAS average composite	77	215.22	243.34	234.41	5.83
Difference between 2001 composite score and 1999–00 average composite	75	–6.07	14.86	0.46	3.40

Note. prof & adv = proficient and advanced performance levels; WyCAS = Wyoming Comprehensive Assessment System.

Table A3

Descriptive Statistics for the Variables Used in This Study: Eleventh Grade

Measure	N	Minimum	Maximum	M	SD
Reading scale score 1999	70	222	252	238.16	6.16
Writing scale score 1999	70	227	256	243.12	6.47
Math scale score 1999	70	214	245	231.68	7.17
Reading scale score 2000	70	226	248	236.93	5.08
Writing scale score 2000	70	223	253	239.57	5.36
Math scale score 2000	70	218	250	233.69	6.12
Reading scale score 2001	73	221	255	238.08	7.35
Writing scale score 2001	73	224	256	241.60	6.77
Math scale score 2001	73	216	249	234.48	7.45
Reading 3-year scale score average	73	222	249	237.33	5.90
Writing 3-year scale score average	73	224	251	241.05	5.79
Math 3-year scale score average	73	216	245	232.95	7.00
Reading 3-year % prof & adv	73	11	75	45.85	12.68
Writing 3-year % prof & adv	73	20	86	55.56	13.73
Math 3-year % prof & adv	73	0	63	35.33	15.01
Building condition score	67	31.49	100	72.23	15.67
Building suitability score	68	20	100	75.79	18.18
Composite scale score 1999	70	221.70	249.52	237.65	6.26
Composite scale score 2000	70	224.51	249.67	236.73	5.09
Composite scale score 2001	73	220.67	252.67	238.05	6.79
1999–01 WyCAS average composite	73	223.82	248.54	237.29	5.61
Difference between 2001 composite score and 1999–00 average composite	69	−11.96	11.11	1.30	4.14

Note. prof & adv = proficient and advanced performance levels; WyCAS = Wyoming Comprehensive Assessment System.

Table A4

Descriptive Statistics for the Variables Used in This Study: All Grades

Measure	N	Minimum	Maximum	M	SD
Reading scale score 1999	301	215.97	252.41	236.11	6.20
Writing scale score 1999	301	217.61	255.54	238.47	7.17
Math scale score 1999	301	207.81	248.78	230.98	7.13
Reading scale score 2000	302	212.62	252.88	234.17	6.69
Writing scale score 2000	302	207.87	253.14	235.43	7.54
Math scale score 2000	302	204.48	250.43	229.71	7.75
Reading scale score 2001	308	214	260	236.39	7.03
Writing scale score 2001	308	218	256	238.33	7.13
Math scale score 2001	308	205	255	231.50	7.89
Reading 3-year scale score average	308	216	255	235.54	6.17
Writing 3-year scale score average	308	218	256	237.34	6.69
Math 3-year scale score average	308	205	256	230.76	7.20
Reading 3-year % prof & adv	308	5	83	45.95	14.13
Writing 3-year % prof & adv	308	10	86	44.63	16.57
Math 3-year % prof & adv	308	0	83	33.33	14.05
Building condition score	296	31.49	100	72.38	14.73
Building suitability score	292	17	100	71.28	18.28
Composite scale score 1999	301	214.45	249.52	235.19	6.23
Composite scale score 2000	302	208.86	249.67	233.10	6.83
Composite scale score 2001	308	213.33	252.67	235.40	6.89
1999–01 WyCAS average composite	308	214.67	251.33	234.60	6.09
Difference between 2001 composite score and 1999–00 average composite	299	−11.96	14.86	1.23	4.23

Note. prof & adv = proficient and advanced performance levels; WyCAS = Wyoming Comprehensive Assessment System.

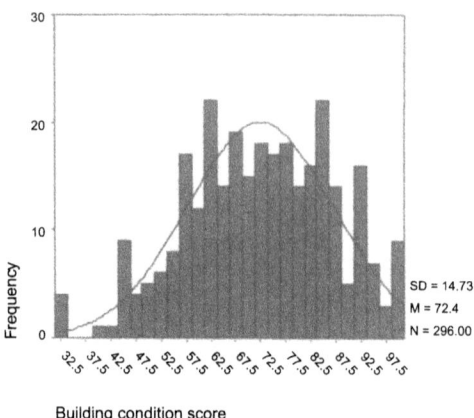

Figure A1. MGT school condition scores.

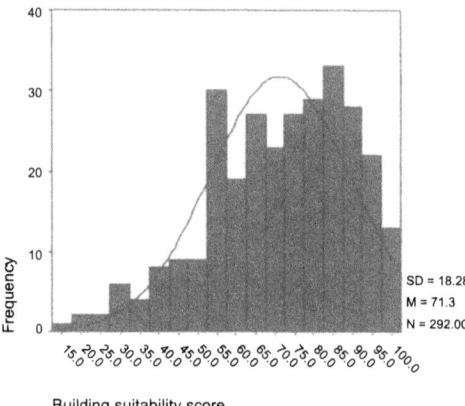

Figure A2. MGT school suitability scores.

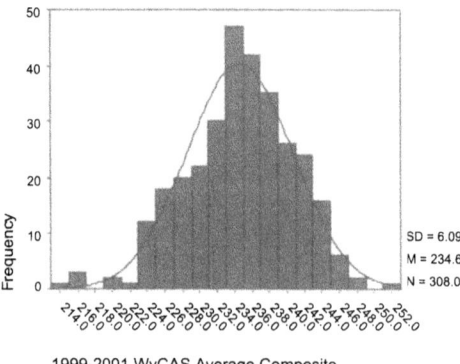

Figure A3. Wyoming Comprehensive Assessment System composite scores.

Appendix B
Additional Correlational Analyses

Table B1

Correlation Between Condition Score and Various Single-Year Achievement

Measure	All Grades[a]	4th Grade[b]	8th Grade[c]	11th Grade[d]
Reading scale score 1999	.02	.01	.03	.05
Writing scale score 1999	.03	.04	.05	.06
Math scale score 1999	.00	.01	.02	−.04
Reading scale score 2000	−.01	−.05	.03	.01
Writing scale score 2000	−.01	.00	.03	−.10
Math scale score 2000	.00	−.02	.00	.02
Reading scale score 2001	−.01	.02	−.05	−.04
Writing scale score 2001	−.04	−.03	−.04	−.06
Math scale score 2001	−.03	.02	−.07	−.09

[a] $n = 296$. [b] $n = 155$. [c] $n = 74$. [d] $n = 67$.

Table B2

Correlation Between Suitability Score and Various Single-Year Achievement

Measures	All Grades[a]	Grade 4[b]	Grade 8[c]	Grade 11[d]
Reading scale score 1999	.15	.09	−.02	.40**
Writing scale score 1999	.21**	.13	.05	.35**
Math scale score 1999	.12*	.09	.01	.32**
Reading scale score 2000	.04	.04	−.08	.07
Writing scale score 2000	.06	.01	−.03	.00
Math scale score 2000	.07	.03	−.11	.16
Reading scale score 2001	.00	.02	−.13	.01
Writing scale score 2001	.00	−.05	−.15	.02
Math scale score 2001	.03	−.01	−.05	.07

[a] $n = 292$. [b] $n = 151$. [c] $n = 73$. [d] $n = 68$.
*$p \leq .05$. **$p \leq .01$.

Assessing the Use of Econometric Analysis in Estimating the Costs of Meeting State Education Accountability Standards: Lessons From Texas

Jennifer Imazeki
Department of Economics
San Diego State University

Andrew Reschovsky
Robert M. La Follette School of Public Affairs
University of Wisconsin–Madison

In 2004, over 300 school districts in Texas challenged the constitutionality of the Texas system of school finance. In *West Orange-Cove et al. v. Neeley et al.*, the plaintiffs argued that because most school districts were at or near a state-imposed property tax rate ceiling and because the share of state education funding was declining, most school districts had inadequate funds to satisfy the student performance standards mandated by the Texas Educational Accountability system. To address the empirical question of whether school districts have insufficient resources to meet the state's accountability standards, two cost function analyses were conducted. One study, entered into evidence by the state of Texas, reached the conclusion that "in aggregate,

Requests for reprints should be sent to Andrew Reschovsky, Robert M. La Follette School of Public Affairs, University of Wisconsin–Madison, 1225 Observatory Drive, Madison, WI 53706. E-mail: reschovsky@lafollette.wisc.edu

the level of education funding in Texas is more than sufficient to meet performance goals consistent with the state's accountability system." The other study, entered into evidence by the plaintiff school districts, concluded that, in aggregate, Texas school districts would need at least $2 billion in additional revenue to satisfy the requirements of the accountability system.

In this article we describe the methodological similarities and differences between the two cost function studies and provide an assessment of why the two studies arrive at such different results. Based on the outcome of the case in district court—a victory for the plaintiffs—the article draws some lessons about the use of statistical-based models in a judicial setting.

With the passage of the No Child Left Behind Act of 2001 (NCLB), all states are required to test students on an annual basis and to ensure that all students make adequate yearly progress (AYP) toward meeting state standards of academic proficiency. In the years prior to the passage of NCLB, courts in a number of states ruled that their systems of public education must be structured so that all children are provided with an adequate education. In these states, the courts, with varying degrees of specificity, have defined the characteristics of an adequate education. It is then left to state legislatures to devise systems of school finance that assure that local school districts have sufficient resources to meet their states' adequacy standards.

State governments throughout the country are being forced to reform their systems of school finance so that all school districts within a state have sufficient resources to meet the rising accountability standards mandated by NCLB and, at least in some states, by court decisions. To have a chance of being successful, these efforts at school finance reform require knowledge about the minimum amount of money needed in each district to meet the academic performance standards. Over the past decade there have been a large number of studies conducted in various states, all designed to provide information to decision makers about the costs of providing what has come to be called an "adequate" education.

Researchers have followed a number of different methodologies in developing estimates of the costs of meeting any given set of education standards. A review of this literature suggests that most studies involve one of three methodological approaches: the professional judgment approach, the successful schools approach, and the cost function (or econometric) approach. For assessments of the advantages and disadvantages of each approach, see Duncombe, Lukemeyer, and Yinger (2004) and Baker, Taylor, and Vedlitz (2004).

Researchers conducting a "professional judgment" study organize several teams of educators within a state and ask them to design an educational program that will achieve the state's educational goals. Once team members have identified the set of inputs required to achieve the stated goals, researchers determine how much money will be needed to fund the specified set of inputs. In many professional judgment studies, members of the panel of experts are also asked about the extra resources that would be required to provide certain types of students, such as those from low-income families, with an adequate education. Cost estimates using the "successful schools" approach start by identifying a set of high-performing schools and then basing estimates of the cost of providing a high-quality education on the lowest level of per-pupil spending among the set of successful schools. Researchers estimating cost functions rely on data from all school districts within a state on per-pupil school expenditures, student performance, and various characteristics of students and school districts. A cost function provides an estimate for each district of the minimum amount of money necessary to achieve various educational performance goals given the characteristics of the school district and its student body. Given that Texas is characterized by a tremendous diversity in both student and school district characteristics, Baker et al. (2004) concluded that conducting a cost function analysis " is the most obvious fit to the challenges of educational cost analysis in Texas" (p. 26).

In this article we describe two cost function studies that were recently conducted in Texas. The explicit purpose of both studies was to determine whether school districts have sufficient resources to meet the state's education accountability standards. Although both studies involved the econometric estimation of cost functions, they reached very different conclusions about the adequacy of education funding in Texas. The results of these two studies are of more than academic interest, as they both played a role in a court case challenging the constitutionality of the system of school finance in Texas. The plaintiffs and intervenors in the court case, *West Orange-Cove et al. v. Neeley et al.* (2004), are a large and diverse group of Texas school districts.[1]

One study, entered into evidence by the state of Texas, reached the conclusion that "in aggregate, the level of education funding in Texas is more than sufficient to meet performance goals consistent with the state's ac-

---

[1]The *West Orange-Cove et al. v. Neeley et al.* (2004) case has a long history. It was originally filed in April 2001 by four high-property wealth districts. After losing in both district court and the appeals court, in May 2003 the Texas Supreme Court reversed the lower courts and sent the case back to district court. The list of plaintiff school districts in the 2004 case has been expanded to include 47 districts representing both rural areas and the state's largest cities. The case was argued in Travis County District Court in a 6-week trial starting in August 2004.

countability system" (Taylor, 2004b, p. 2). The other study, entered into evidence by the plaintiff school districts, concluded that, in aggregate, Texas school districts would need at least $2 billion in additional revenue to satisfy the requirements of the accountability system.

Both studies used cost function methodology and similar data, but as discussed in greater detail later, they differed with respect to several specification and estimation issues. The first study, issued in March 2004 by Timothy Gronberg, Dennis Jansen, Lori Taylor, and Kevin Booker (hereafter referred to as GJTB), was originally conducted for the Texas Joint Select Committee on Public School Finance. The cost function estimation in that study was based primarily on earlier work by Gronberg and Jansen that was part of a larger project, undertaken at the request of the legislature by the Charles A. Dana Center at the University of Texas–Austin to analyze variations in educational costs (Alexander et al., 2000).

The second study, by Jennifer Imazeki and Andrew Reschovsky (2004a; hereafter referred to as IR), was undertaken at the request of the West Orange-Cove plaintiffs. The cost function estimation in that study was based largely on earlier Texas cost function studies by the authors, conducted as academic research (Imazeki & Reschovsky, 2004b; Reschovsky & Imazeki, 2003). Although the studies were conducted independently, to facilitate comparisons between the two studies, the cost predictions in both studies were based on similar academic performance standards.

In the next section of this article, we briefly describe the system of school finance in Texas. As we explain, even if the Texas Supreme Court reverses the district court ruling in *West Orange-Cove et al. v. Neeley et al.* (2004), there is widespread agreement in Texas that the school funding system is in crisis and will need to be reformed. In the following section, we explain the major elements of the judicial challenge to the system. We explain the evidentiary role played by the two cost function studies and briefly indicate how these studies influenced the ruling of the judge in the case. In the next section, we provide a primer on the basics of the cost function approach to the estimation of the costs of achieving an adequate education. This is followed by a section in which we describe and evaluate the different assumptions and approaches taken by the two cost function studies. We then discuss the contrasting ways in which the two studies use their cost function results to generate estimates of the amount of money needed by school districts in Texas to meet the student performance standards mandated by the Texas accountability system. In the final section of the article, we attempt to draw some general conclusions about the use of cost function analysis in providing estimates of the costs of educational adequacy.

School Finance in Texas

The school finance system in Texas has been shaped by legislative response to a long series of court challenges to the Texas educational finance system.[2] The current system was established in 1993 and was designed to satisfy a series of previous court rulings that had declared the system of education finance unconstitutional. In January 1995, the Texas Supreme Court ruled that the school funding system established in 1993 satisfied constitutional muster. Although there have been some small revisions to the school funding formulas since then, the basic system of state aid remains in place today.

The school funding system is a complex assortment of formulas, adjustments, and weights collectively known as the Foundation School Program (FSP). The three most important elements of the system include (a) a foundation formula (Tier I), which guarantees all school districts a certain amount of money if they agree to levy a minimum property tax rate; (b) a guaranteed tax base formula (Tier II), which guarantees all districts a fixed amount of money for each cent of additional property tax rate above the minimum and below a statutory maximum; and (c) a recapture provision, which caps the revenue-raising capacity of all property-wealthy districts by requiring them to contribute all property tax revenues on property values above the caps to help finance the FSP. This last provision has resulted in the school finance system frequently being described as a Robin Hood system of education finance.

For the 2004–05 school year, the Tier I foundation level called the *basic allotment*, was set at $2,537 per student. This amount was adjusted for each school district to reflect small district size, geographical sparsity, and a cost of education index that reflects differences across districts in factors such as the cost of living and the concentration of low-income students. Each school district's Tier I and Tier II allocations are further adjusted to reflect differences in student characteristics by assigning additional "weights" to students in special education, compensatory education, bilingual education, vocational education, and gifted and talented programs.

In 2004–05, Tier II guarantees each district $27.14 per weighted pupil for each additional penny of property tax rate between the required minimum rate of $0.86 per $100 of assessed value and the statutory limit of $1.50. School districts with property wealth between the Tier II guaranteed tax base of $271,400 per pupil and $305,000 are free to raise additional property tax revenue (as long as their tax rate remains below the $1.50 cap). Dis-

---

[2]For a brief history of school finance litigation in Texas, see Imazeki and Reschovsky (2004b).

tricts with property wealth above $305,000 per pupil are required to share all property tax revenue generated by property values in excess of $305,000.

The Judicial Challenge to the Constitutionality of School Finance in Texas

School finance reform has been a major topic of public discourse in Texas in 2004. In March, the legislature's Joint Select Committee on Public School Finance issued a final report in which they recommended a number of major changes to the school finance system. In April, Governor Perry called a 1-month special session of the legislature to deal with school finance. The central focus of the special session was on the financing of a major reduction in school property taxes and a repeal of the recapture provision of the current school funding system. Due to its inability to agree on a new source of revenue, the special session ended without the enactment of any new legislation. Finally, in August over 300 Texas school districts joined together as plaintiffs and interveners in a court case, *West Orange-Cove et al. v. Neeley et al.* (2004), challenging the constitutionality of the current system of school finance. In late November 2004, the Travis County District Court's presiding judge, John Dietz, issued a ruling in which he declared the Texas school funding system to be unconstitutional. He gave the legislature until October 1, 2005 to come up with a new funding system that remedied the constitutional violations. Immediately following Judge Dietz's ruling, Texas Attorney General Greg Abbot indicated his intention to appeal directly to the Texas Supreme Court.

To understand the legislature's and the governor's interest in school finance reform, and the basis of the plaintiffs' arguments in the *West Orange-Cove* case, it is necessary to describe several elements of the school finance system and explain how they are forcing changes in the system of school finance. The first element is the state's falling share of education funding. In 2000, the state financed 47% of school funding. Four years later, the state's share had fallen to 38%. The reason for the falling state share of FSP funding is that neither the state's foundation nor its guaranteed tax base formulas are automatically adjusted for the rising costs of education. In fact, the basic allotment has not been raised in 5 years, and the guaranteed tax base was last increased in 2002–03. Therefore, as per-pupil property values grow from one year to the next, both Tier I and Tier II state aid allocations are reduced. As a result, many school districts have been forced to raise their property tax rates, both to make up reductions in state aid and to meet rising education costs.

The ability of school districts in Texas to raise their property tax rates is limited, however, by a state statute that prohibits property tax rates for maintenance and operating expenses in excess of $1.50 per $100 of assessed value (15 mills).[3] For the 2003–04 school year, 828 of the 1,031 school districts in Texas had rates above $1.40, with the majority of them already at the $1.50 cap.[4] From their public pronouncements, it is clear that a very important priority for both Governor Perry and for many members of the legislature is to find a way to substantially reduce school property tax rates. In fact, in their final report, the legislature's Joint Special Committee on Public School Finance concluded that one of the primary goals of school finance reform should be provision of "significant" property tax relief, which the committee defined as property tax rate reductions of at least $0.50 per $100 of valuation.

In addition to providing general property tax relief, the repeal of the "recapture" provision of the school finance system is a high priority of the governor and of many members of the legislature. Over the past decade, the state has failed to adjust the Equalized Wealth Level (the per-student property value above which all property wealth must be shared) to the growth in property values. As a consequence, each year more school districts are subject to the recapture provisions. Those school districts subject to recapture are very tightly constrained in their ability to increase education spending, regardless of whether the increased spending is due to uncontrollable costs caused by enrollment growth, rising accountability standards, or other factors.

The final, and perhaps most controversial, factor that is driving school finance reform is the rising cost of meeting Texas accountability standards. The upward pressure on costs comes from three sources. First, accountability standards are rising over time. Not only has Texas replaced its testing system, the Texas Assessment of Academic Skills (TAAS), with a new and more difficult set of tests called the Texas Assessment of Knowledge and Skills (TAKS), but NCLB requires that the percentage of students passing the tests at a level considered to be "proficient" increase each year over the next decade. In addition, Texas has adopted new, broader curriculum standards and has imposed tougher grade promotion and graduation requirements. It is difficult to imagine that these higher expectations from the public school system can be met without the annual expenditure of addi-

---

[3]School districts are also able to levy a separate property tax rate, limited to $0.50, for the purpose of meeting debt payments associated with school buildings.

[4]School districts with property tax rates above $1.40 in 2003–04 collectively educated 90% of public school students in Texas.

tional funds. One goal of the two cost function studies was to provide estimates of these additional costs.

The second reason the costs of education are rising over time is due to the steady increase in the number of students that the public education system in Texas must educate. Although enrollments in many parts of the country are projected to decline over the next decade, projections by the National Center for Education Statistics (2003) indicate that Texas will experience an average growth in public school enrollment of about 1% per year over the next decade.

The third reason that the costs of education are rising is that the composition of the student body is changing over time. Enrollment data from the Texas Education Agency (TEA) indicate that in recent years most of the net growth in public school enrollment has come from growth in the number of students from low-income and minority families. According to the Texas state demographer, if current demographic trends continue, the student body in Texas will continue to become more Hispanic and more low income (Murdock et al., 2003). The weight of evidence from a large literature on the costs of education, including the findings of both the GJTB and the IR studies, indicate that the costs of meeting educational accountability standards are substantially higher when a high proportion of students come from economically disadvantaged families and enter schools with limited English proficiency (LEP). Therefore, school districts in Texas will face increased pressure to raise spending not only because of the growth in the number of students but also because their student bodies will, over time, include higher concentrations of students who are relatively expensive to educate.

In bringing their case challenging the constitutionality of the current school funding system in Texas, the plaintiff districts argued that the $1.50 statutory property tax cap has become both a floor and a ceiling for most school districts and that, under the current funding system, school districts do not have access to sufficient resources to provide a constitutionally mandated "general diffusion of knowledge." The plaintiffs argued that because of the falling share of state aid and the rising costs of meeting state accountability standards, school districts have lost all "meaningful discretion" over their property tax rates. Furthermore, because so many school districts have reached the $1.50 rate cap, the school property tax has become a de facto state ad valorem property tax, something that is constitutionally prohibited in Texas. The plaintiffs also presented evidence, based on the IR study and on a "professional judgment study" completed by James Smith and Richard Seder (2004), that most school districts must increase spending to be able to meet the state's accountability standards and satisfy the constitutionally mandated requirement that they provide an adequate education. They argued that the school finance system is unconstitutional because it fails to provide school districts with access to sufficient resources to enable to them to provide an adequate education.

Having a good estimate of the cost of an adequate education, namely the amount of money needed to satisfy the general diffusion of knowledge clause of the constitution, was critically important for both the plaintiffs and the state. If the costs of providing an adequate education and meeting all other state and federal education mandates were clearly below the level of current spending, then the state could argue that local school districts had the ability to lower their current property tax rates to levels that were substantially below the $1.50 cap and still provide for the general diffusion of knowledge. On the other hand, if the cost of providing a constitutionally adequate education to the public school students of Texas requires additional spending beyond the current spending levels, then not only would school districts have no meaningful discretion to lower their tax rates but, given the current level of state funding, they would have no means of satisfying the state's educational accountability standards and the constitutional requirement to provide for the general diffusion of knowledge.

Although, as we discuss later in this article, both of the cost function studies were based on a set of several student performance measures, the single most important outcome measure used in both studies was the passing rate on the mathematics and reading exams that are part of a set of standardized exams that nearly all students must take, the TAKS. Once one has estimated a cost function, it is easy to use the cost function results to calculate the costs, for individual districts and across the entire state, of meeting any reasonable passing rate standard. The GJTB study calculated the costs of education for a single standard, an average composite passing rate on the two exams of 55%. GJTB argued that the 55% passing rate provides a reasonable measure of an adequate education, one that provides for the general diffusion of knowledge.[5] They justified the 55% passing rate as an appropriate standard by pointing out that the TEA has set as its goal a 53.5% passing rate for the reading and language arts exam and 41.7% passing rate for the mathematics exam. GJTB predicted that the cost of assuring that all districts achieve a 55% average passing rate on the two exams, and that districts that are already at

---

[5] As we discuss later, the plaintiffs in the *West Orange-Cove et al. v. Neeley et al.* (2004) case argued that both the test score that students need to pass the exams and the 55% standard are too low to be considered appropriate measures of an adequate education.

or above the 55% standard improve their passing rate by 2.87 percentage points, equals $6,403 per pupil (in 2004 dollars).[6]

To provide a cost comparison with GJTB, IR also calculated costs on the basis of a 55% passing rate standard. Their estimated cost per pupil is $7,518 per student—over $1,100 per pupil higher than the GJTB estimate.[7] Adding these two predictions over Texas's 4.3 million public school students results in an estimate of $26.1 billion of total predicted costs by GJTB and $30.9 billion by IR, a difference that is equivalent to 18% of total public school revenue in 2003–04.

The Use of Cost Functions to Measure the Costs on an Adequate Education

In both studies, the primary empirical question was whether school districts have sufficient resources to meet the state's accountability standards. This can be broken down into two separate questions. First, how much does it cost for any given district to meet the state's accountability standards? Once that is established, does the current system provide enough funding to cover those costs, or is additional money needed? To answer the first question, both studies estimated cost functions for K–12 education in Texas.

Cost functions provide a practical way to identify and quantify the factors that influence the costs of education, where the *output* of school districts can be measured using multiple measures of student performance. By estimating a cost function based on data on K–12 school districts, we can characterize in detail the relation between spending per pupil by school districts and various measures of student performance while also taking account of the characteristics of each school district's student body; other characteristics of the school district, such as size; and the prices the school district must pay for inputs into the education process.

In algebraic terms, a cost function can be represented by the following equation:

$$E_{it} = h(S_{it}, P_{it}, Z_{it}, F_{it}, \varepsilon_{it}, u_{it}), \tag{1}$$

[6]That is, for districts with passing rates already at or above 52.13% (55.0 − 2.87), the predicted cost reflects the cost of improving their passing rate by 2.87 percentage points. For districts that were below 52.13%, the predicted cost reflects the cost of getting up to the 55% standard.

[7]Both these estimates are based on school operating expenses and exclude all spending on transportation and food services.

where per-pupil expenditures, E_{it}, are specified as a function of public school outputs; S_{it}, a vector of input prices; P_{it}, the characteristics of the student body; Z_{it}, other characteristics of the school district, such as its size; F_{it}, a vector of unobserved characteristics of the school district, e_{it}; and a random error term, u_{it}. Once a functional form is chosen for Equation 1, it can be estimated with district-level data for a given state. The resulting coefficients indicate the contribution of various district characteristics to the cost of education, holding constant the level of output. These cost function results can then be used to predict the cost of any given level of performance on the included outcome variables. These predictions are generated by multiplying the cost function coefficients by the actual values of the student and district characteristics while holding the output variables constant at the desired level. For the *West Orange-Cove* case specifically, the GJTB and IR studies used their respective cost functions to predict the costs associated with the performance standards set out in the Texas accountability system.

In any empirical analysis, there are a number of choices that the researcher must make. For example, before estimating Equation 1 one must first specify a functional form (e.g., linear, log linear, etc.). Choices must be made about which student performance, school district, and student characteristics to include, as well as how to define those variables. Although these choices are guided by an underlying model of public decision making and assumptions about cost minimization, researchers still have considerable latitude in choosing specific variables and functional forms. Furthermore, in the real world, some schools may fail to minimize costs; hence, they may operate inefficiently. Although these potential inefficiencies are not directly observed, researchers can follow different strategies in an attempt to address school district inefficiencies. Public finance economists also generally assume that school district spending decisions have a direct impact on student performance goals, and decisions about what goals to meet have direct implications for the level of per-pupil spending a district must undertake. Therefore, researchers must make decisions about how to account for this simultaneous relation between per-pupil spending and student outcome.

Each of these choices has implications for the final cost function results and any subsequent cost predictions that are derived from those results. The authors of the IR and GJTB studies estimated a version of Equation 1, and in certain respects, their results were qualitatively similar. Both studies found that costs increase with the percentage of low-income, LEP, and disabled students as well as finding higher costs for small districts and for districts that must pay higher teacher salaries. In almost all cases, however, the estimated effects are smaller in the GJTB analysis. This is due, in part, to the different choices made by the authors with regard to a number of the estimation issues mentioned earlier and discussed in greater detail in the next section.

How the Two Cost Functions Studies Differ

In this section, we discuss some of the major differences between the two studies in the specification and estimation of a cost function for K–12 education in Texas.

Measuring Test Scores

As noted by Baker et al. (2004), "a central difficulty of performance-oriented analysis involves the politics of achieving consensus regarding *important outcomes* and the empirics of precisely measuring those outcomes" (p. 20). Fortunately, for the most part, the choice of outcomes and the measurement of those outcomes have already been made in Texas. The Texas accountability system is built around a set of standardized tests. Since the early 1990s, Texas has had a well-developed testing system for the majority of its students. Until 2002–03, all students in Grades 3 through 8 and in Grade 10 were tested in the spring of each year as part of the TAAS. In 2002–03, the TAAS was replaced with the TAKS, a more rigorous test, and testing was extended to students in Grades 9 and 11. Passing rates on the TAKS are the primary basis for assessing the performance of schools and school districts as part of the Texas accountability system.

Both the GJTB and IR studies included test scores as an outcome measure—specifically, changes in passing rates in reading and math on the TAAS for students in Grades 5 through 8 and 10. It is appropriate to focus on *changes* in student performance (as opposed to *levels*) in estimating a cost function because a primary objective of schools is to improve, on an annual basis, the knowledge and skills of students. An additional reason for using a "value-added" measure of student performance is that both NCLB and Texas accountability standards call for students to make AYP toward the achievement of the accountability standards. To generate a value-added measure of test scores, however, it was necessary to use scores from the TAAS because multiple years of data on the TAKS were not available.

Unfortunately, using data from the TAAS presents a problem for any analysis of the state's accountability standards because those standards are based on performance on the TAKS exams. As mentioned earlier, the TAKS exams are more rigorous than the TAAS exams, and scores on the two exams are not directly comparable. To further complicate matters, the state is phasing in passing standards on the TAKS, increasing the score required to pass each year.[8] Therefore, a given passing rate in 2003 still represents a lower level of performance than the same passing rate in 2005 because the individual score needed to pass is higher in 2005.

To predict costs associated with performance on the TAKS, each study took a somewhat different approach. In the GJTB study, the cost function was estimated with changes in TAAS passing rates. The resulting coefficient on the test score variable thus reflects the marginal effect of a 1 percentage point increase in the TAAS passing rate. Those coefficients are then used to predict the cost of achieving changes in passing rates on the TAKS. This assumes that the cost of achieving a 1 percentage point increase in the passing rate on the TAKS (regardless of the cut score) is the same as the cost of achieving a 1 percentage point increase in the passing rate on the TAAS. If improvements on the TAKS are more (or less) costly than improvements on the TAAS, then this assumption will lead to lower (or higher) predictions of the costs of achieving standards on the TAKS.

In the IR study, the cost function was estimated using a measure of the TAAS scores that had been converted to the TAKS standards. The conversion is based on a conversion schedule developed by the TEA, which indicates how a given score on the TAAS correlates to expected performance on the TAKS; at the 2005 cut scores, that is, a student would need a particular TAAS score to have passed the TAKS at the passing standard in place for 2005. Because the cost function is estimated with converted passing rates, the resulting coefficient on the test score variable reflects the marginal effect of a 1 percentage point increase in the TAKS passing rate, at the 2005 cut scores, and can be used directly to predict the cost of improvements on the TAKS. This approach, however, relies heavily on the accuracy of TEA's TAAS–TAKS conversion.

Measuring Value Added

Whether converted to TAKS scores or not, both studies use a value-added measure of TAAS performance, comparing passing rates in 2001–02 with passing rates in a previous year. Therefore, each study estimates the cost of achieving a certain *gain* in passing rates. GJTB used a

---

[8]Note that there are several elements involved in determining standards for these exams: First is the decision of what grade on any examination will be considered passing (which we refer to as the "cut score"), and second are the passing rates, or the increase in passing rates, that are considered high enough to meet the standard (which we refer to as the "passing rate" standard). Between 2002 and 2005, the state accountability system is increasing the cut scores; after 2005, the passing rate standard will increase each year.

2-year lag, and they matched passing rates in 2001–02 for Grades 5 through 8 and 10 with passing rates for the same students 2 years earlier (1999–00), when those students were in Grades 3 through 6 and 8.[9] The coefficient on the test score variable thus reflects the marginal effect of a 1 percentage point increase on the TAAS over a 2-year period. However, GJTB's dependent variable, per-pupil expenditures, was for the 2001–02 school year, and the predicted costs were presented as annual costs. However, as Lori Taylor (2004c, pp. 54–55) pointed out at the trial, the coefficient estimated by GJTB was, at best, only one half of the marginal effect of a 1-year gain. To see this, take two equations: $y = a + bx$ and $y = a + c(x/2)$. For a given x, b must be equal to $c/2$. If x is a 2-year gain in test scores (as in the GJTB estimation), and x/2 is a 1-year gain (assuming the gain is equal in each year, which may, in itself, be a strong assumption), the coefficient in the GJTB estimation (i.e., b) is only half of the marginal effect of a 1-year gain (i.e., c). This implies that the GJTB study probably underestimates the cost of achieving a given *annual* improvement in test scores.

IR used a 1-year lag and matched passing rates in 2001–02 for Grades 5 through 8 and 10 to passing rates in 2000–01 for Grades 3 through 8 and 10. Given available data, this was the only way to have a 1-year lag. The resulting variables, however, do not exactly match the same cohort of students. This fact may create statistical noise, and perhaps bias, in the resulting estimates, although the direction of that bias is not clear (i.e., it may lead to under- or overestimates of the marginal effects).

Pupil Weighting

Because the dependent variable in a cost function is per-pupil spending, and available data on spending is almost always at the district level, cost functions are estimated with variables aggregated to the district level (percentage of students from low-income families, percentage disabled, etc.). The data thus represent average characteristics of each district. Using this kind of data may be problematic, however, when those averages are calculated over districts of varying sizes. This is certainly likely in a state such as Texas, where there are vast differences in district size. For example, Houston ISD, the state's largest district, serves over 210,000 students, whereas there are 343 school districts with enrollments of less than 500 students. The 775 smallest Texas districts educate only 20% of public school students, whereas another 20% of students are educated in the state's 8 largest districts.

---

[9]Their measure does not include any students who drop out during those 2 years or any who enter the Texas schools during that time.

Using data that represent averages for districts of such varying sizes may lead to a common econometric problem, known as *heteroskedasticity*.[10] A quite standard way to account for this problem is by weighting each observation by group (district) size. This was the approach taken by IR. As a result, their estimated cost function coefficients reflected the cost relations that exist for the average student in the state. Pupil weighting means that each of the larger districts contributes more information to the estimation than each small district. The authors argued that this is appropriate because the majority of students are educated in relatively large districts.

GJTB also accounted for heteroskedasticity in their estimation, but they used a different econometric technique and did not pupil weight. Because the GJTB study did not pupil weight, their cost function results still reflected the relationships between per-pupil spending, student performance, and student characteristics in the average district. The consequence of not pupil weighting is that a very small district contributes the same amount of information to the estimation as an extremely large district. Because there are so many small districts, this means that the relationship between spending and district size is easier to identify among small districts. However, because there are only a few large districts, there is more "noise" in the estimation, and any relation between spending and district size will be more difficult to identify among large districts. This may lead to an overemphasis on the relationship between spending and small district size but an understatement of the relationship between spending and large district size.

Teacher Salaries

Teacher salaries account for the largest share of school expenditures and are arguably the most important input in the educational process. Any educational cost function must therefore include some measure of the price of this input. However, the goal of cost function analysis is to isolate factors that contribute to higher spending but are outside the control of local school districts. However, districts make decisions about the quality of teachers that they recruit, and those decisions can affect spending levels. Teacher salary levels are also generally determined through a process of negotiation with teacher organizations, and school boards have a substantial impact on the outcome of these negotiations. Therefore, rather than using actual teacher salaries, it is more appropriate to use a measure of teacher salaries that minimizes the influence of school district decisions.

---

[10]Heteroskedasticity refers to a situation where the error term cannot be considered random.

In estimating their cost function, GJTB used the average salary for beginning teachers in a district (those with less than 5 years' experience). They pointed out that this "is a better measure of the wage level in a district than the average wage paid to all teachers because beginning teacher wages are less influenced by differences in the experience profiles of districts" (p. 10). They also included the average salary of teacher aides and auxiliary personnel. However, because actual wages are subject to district control, GJTB's estimated effect of salaries on spending may have been biased downward.

IR instead used an index of teacher costs developed by Taylor (2004a). Her index separated variations in compensation arising from uncontrollable district characteristics (such as area cost of living) from variations arising from factors that districts can influence (such as teacher experience and educational background). Therefore, the estimated coefficient reflects the higher spending associated with only those salary costs that are outside the control of the local district.

Functional Form

Both studies estimated some version of Equation 1 but must first specify a functional form for that equation. IR estimated a log-linear model in which continuous variables, other than variables measured as percentages, are transformed by taking natural logarithms. To capture possible economies and diseconomies of scale, they also included quadratic (squared) terms for the percentage of LEP students, percentage of severely disabled students, and the log of district enrollment. In their model, the coefficients on most variables can be interpreted directly as the marginal effect of a one-unit change in the variable.[11] The resulting coefficients are then used to predict the costs of achieving any given level of student performance.

GJTB estimated a *translog* model in which continuous variables, other than variables measured as percentages, are transformed by taking natural logarithms, all of the variables are interacted with (multiplied by) all other variables, and quadratic terms for all variables are also included.[12] This is a very flexible specification, but the flexibility comes at the cost of complexity. The model GJTB estimated has 109 independent variables (compared to 19 in the IR specification), and the numerous interactions and quadratic

---

[11]With the three variables for which quadratic terms are also included, the marginal effects must be calculated from the coefficients on both the variable itself and the quadratic term; therefore, this will change with the level of the variable.

[12]The Gronberg, Jansen, Taylor, and Booker (2004) model also included a cubic term for district enrollment.

terms make the resulting coefficients much harder to interpret. Also, it is much more difficult to assess the impact of a change in any one variable on per-pupil spending while holding other variables constant. The presence of the interaction terms means that these so-called *marginal effects* will depend on the value of the variable of interest and the values of all the other variables. For example, the impact on per-pupil spending of a 1 percentage point increase in the percentage of poor students in a district will depend on school district size, on the salary of beginning teachers, on the percentage of a district's students enrolled in high school, plus the other cost factors and outcome variables included in the cost function.

Rather than exploiting the full flexibility inherent in the translog functional form, GJTB chose to calculate the marginal effects of each cost factor on per-pupil spending by setting the value of all variables equal to their average values. These calculated marginal effects were then used to predict costs.[13] This approach has the advantage of being relatively easy to explain. The cost of using this simpler specification, however, is that one loses much of the potential advantage of estimating a cost function with a more flexible form than the log-linear specification used by IR. Because the converted coefficients are the marginal effects calculated at the averages, using the converted specification will lead to lower predicted costs for some districts and higher predicted costs for others, relative to using the translog coefficients directly. The net impact on estimated total costs is unclear.

Efficiency

It is very difficult to determine whether any given school district is operating efficiently. At a conceptual level, a school or school district is operating efficiently if it meets its stated educational goals while spending as little money as possible. Although the concept of cost minimization is straightforward, the actual measurement of efficiency is complicated because it is exceedingly difficult to identify and quantify both the goals of each school district and all the factors that influence the achievement of those goals and contribute to school district spending. Despite these difficulties, it is important that any attempt to measure the costs of meeting student performance goals deducts from costs any spending that is inefficient, namely, spending that does not contribute to achieving those goals.

Given that inefficiencies cannot be directly observed, any analyst faces the problem of finding an indirect way to identify the magnitude of ineffi-

---

[13]That is, they take the translog results and condense them to create a simpler log-linear equation with one term for each variable and coefficients that reflect the marginal effects evaluated at the average values of all variables.

cient spending in each school district. Therefore, it is not surprising that the authors of the two cost function studies use quite different approaches to the measurement of efficiency.

GJTB accounted for school district inefficiency by estimating their cost function with a *stochastic frontier*. This technique considers all spending by a school district that is in excess of estimated minimum costs to be inefficient. The stochastic frontier procedure allowed the authors to identify the minimum level of spending among school districts with similar characteristics and similar levels of student performance. Among the set of similar districts, all spending that is in excess of minimum spending is considered to be inefficient; hence, it is not counted in the calculation of costs.

GJTB correctly pointed out that one must view this efficiency measure with caution. They recognized that efficiency measured using the stochastic frontier is sensitive to the way that school district output is defined. School district spending associated with outputs other than those explicitly included in the cost function estimation will be counted as inefficient. For example, resources that school districts devote to vocational education or arts and music subjects not directly measured by scores on math and reading exams will be classified as inefficient spending. This misclassification is particularly troublesome because state-imposed curriculum requirements mandate that school districts provide students with courses in subjects beyond the core academic subjects—for example, art and music.

The stochastic frontier model may also misclassify spending as inefficient because the cost function estimation is unable to measure the impact of some important "inputs" in the educational process. For example, parental involvement, whether by volunteering in the schools or by helping children with homework, may be an important factor in improving student test scores. This implies that a school district with extensive parental involvement will have lower measured costs and will thus define the frontier spending level for districts with similar characteristics, yet less parental involvement. By definition, higher spending in districts with relatively less parental involvement will be classified as inefficient, despite the fact that the school district has little control over the behavior of the parents of their students.

GJTB recognized that their stochastic frontier analysis systematically overestimates inefficiency; therefore, they based their cost estimates on their average estimated level of inefficiency. However, as their underlying estimate of inefficiency was at best very imprecise, their resulting predictions of costs provided an imprecise measure of the costs of meeting the state's accountability standards. Nevertheless, using the GJTB results, Taylor (2004b) presented point estimates of the inefficiency of individual school districts, for example, showing that about 11% of the Austin school district spending is inefficient. In a recent article, however, Street (2003) demonstrated that efficiency estimates based on stochastic frontier methods are highly sensitive to estimation decisions and argued that little confidence should be placed in the resulting estimates of inefficiency when applied to individual units such as school districts or hospitals.

IR used a completely different approach in their attempt to estimate the impact of school district inefficiency. Rather than attempting to measure efficiency directly, IR assumed that school districts would operate more efficiently if they operate in a competitive local educational market. Although this assumption may be considered controversial, after reviewing a number of studies of government competition, Taylor (2000) concluded that "almost across the board, researchers have found that school spending is lower, academic outcomes are better, and school-district efficiency is higher where parents have more choice in their children's education provider" (p. 7). To measure public school competition, a county-level Herfindahl index is constructed.[14] The index increases with the amount of competition; therefore, if district efficiency is correlated with the amount of competition that the district faces, then spending should be lower in districts with higher values of the Herfindahl index. In predicting costs, IR held the value of the Herfindahl index constant at a relatively high level of efficiency. It is important to point out that, as with the GJTB model, this method does not explicitly capture spending on public school outputs other than those included in the estimation. However, using the Herfindahl index, spending directed to other outcomes, such as music courses, is picked up in each school district's random error term; thus, it is not classified as "inefficient."

Estimation Methods

As mentioned earlier, school districts make decisions about spending levels and student outcome levels simultaneously. That is, although decisions by local school boards to raise the level of student performance presumably will require additional spending, decisions concerning

---

[14]A Herfindahl index for school districts in county k can be calculated using the following formula:

$$\text{Herfindahl Index} = 1 - \sum_i \left(\frac{enrollment_i}{enrollment_k} \right)^2$$

For a county with just one district and no competition, the index will equal zero. For a county with n equally sized districts, the index will equal $1 - 1/n$. Therefore, the index approaches 1 as the number of districts, and presumably competition, increases. This construction assumes that counties can be used to define local "markets" for education.

per-student spending are likely to directly influence student performance. If not appropriately addressed, this simultaneity can lead to bias in estimation of the cost function coefficients, implying that the estimated values of the coefficients may be systematically larger or smaller than the "true" values. One of the more common statistical techniques to deal with potential simultaneity is *two-stage least squares* estimation. This estimation procedure was used by IR. It requires that the analyst find variables, referred to as *instruments*, which are correlated with the student performance measures but are not correlated with school district spending. The advantage of using two-stage least squares is that it removes the bias created by the simultaneous relation among variables and thus provides more confidence that the coefficients reflect the true relations. On the other hand, the use of two-stage least squares may result in a reduction in the statistical significance of some of the estimated coefficients of the cost function.

The GJTB study did not address the simultaneity issue. The authors argued that they ran statistical tests to check for the existence of bias and, on the basis of the test results, concluded that adjustments for simultaneity bias were not necessary. However, the complexity of the translog functional form, combined with the stochastic frontier estimation, would most likely make identification of bias more difficult with the standard tests. Therefore, there is still the possibility that the GJTB coefficient estimates are biased.

Differences in Predicted Costs From the Two Cost Function Studies

The previous section outlined a number of ways in which the two cost function analyses differ. Not surprisingly, each of these differences contributes to differences in the magnitudes and distribution of the predicted costs of meeting any given student performance standard. As mentioned previously, the GJTB study predicted that the cost of all districts achieving a composite passing rate of 55% on the reading and mathematics exams is $6,403 per pupil (in 2004 dollars). Using a slightly different definition of the 55% standard, IR calculated costs of $7,518 per student. Not only do the two studies predict different costs, but they differ considerably in their prediction of which districts have relatively high costs and which districts have relatively low costs. To compare predicted costs across districts, both studies calculate *cost indexes* by using their cost function results to predict the cost of meeting the 55% passing rate standard for each school district as well as the cost of achieving that standard in a district with average values for all the cost factors. The index is the ratio of these two numbers. The index values thus provide a measure of a school district's costs relative to the average district. For example, an index value of 1.25 indicates that a district has predicted costs that are 25% higher than in the average cost district.

As a means of comparing the distribution of the cost indexes generated by the two studies, we have divided school districts into quintiles defined in terms of the percentage of poor students in each district and district size. In defining quintiles, we weight districts by student enrollment so that each quintile contains 20% (one fifth) of all Texas K–12 students. Therefore, the first poverty quintile in Table 1 includes the 133 districts with the lowest percentage of poor students, and these districts enroll approximately 20% of all public school students. Tables 1 and 2 both display for the two studies the average cost index value in each quintile and the minimum and maximum cost index value in each quintile.

As clearly shown in Table 1, both studies indicate that the costs of meeting the accountability standard are higher in districts with heavier concentrations of students from poor families. The IR study, however, found that poverty is a much more important factor contributing to high costs than did the GJTB study. The average cost index associated with the IR study is 1.19 in the fourth poverty quintile and 1.39 in the highest quintile. This contrasts with the much lower average cost index values produced by the GJTB study—1.09 in both the fourth and fifth poverty quintiles.

Table 2 displays the cost index values by district size quintile. It demonstrates that although both studies find a substantial variation in costs in each district size quintile, the IR study predicted that costs would be higher than average in both the smallest and the largest districts. This prediction contrasts with that of the GJTB study, which found that, with the exception of the smallest size quintile of school districts, the value of the average cost index is below average. The difference between the two studies is particularly striking among the state's largest districts, where IR calculated an average cost index of 1.02 (slightly above average); GJTB calculated an average cost index value of 0.87 (substantially below average). As we discussed previously, these different predictions are probably due to the fact that GJTB chose to estimate their cost function without the use of pupil weights.

How the Studies Differ in Assessing Educational Adequacy in Texas

By providing estimates of the amount of money each district needs to meet the state's accountability standards, the two cost function studies answer one of the questions before the court in the *West Orange-Cove et al. v.*

Table 1
Cost Index Values by Poverty Quintiles

Student Weighted Quintiles	No. of School Districts	IR Cost Index Value			GJTB Cost Index Value		
		Average	Minimum	Maximum	Average	Minimum	Maximum
1 (lowest)	133	0.73	0.53	1.03	0.86	0.72	1.21
2	256	0.88	0.67	1.56	0.96	0.78	1.60
3	283	0.98	0.72	1.69	1.01	0.79	1.50
4	214	1.19	0.81	2.65	1.09	0.84	1.70
5 (highest)	82	1.39	0.93	3.54	1.09	0.74	1.99
Total	968	1.00	0.53	3.54	1.00	0.72	1.99

Note. IR = Imazeki and Reschovsky (2004a); GJTB = Gronberg, Jansen, Taylor, and Booker (2004).

Table 2
Cost Index Values by District Size Quintiles

Student Weighted Quintiles	No. of School Districts	IR Cost Index Value			GJTB Cost Index Value		
		Average	Minimum	Maximum	Average	Minimum	Maximum
1 (smallest)	775	1.03	0.55	3.54	1.04	0.77	1.99
2	125	0.87	0.53	1.40	0.85	0.72	1.07
3	40	0.92	0.54	1.17	0.86	0.72	1.02
4	20	0.84	0.61	1.33	0.82	0.75	0.91
5 (largest)	8	1.02	0.69	1.32	0.87	0.77	0.93
Total	968	1.00	0.53	3.54	1.00	0.72	1.99

Note. IR = Imazeki and Reschovsky (2004a); GJTB = Gronberg, Jansen, Taylor, and Booker (2004).

Neeley et al. (2004) case. The answer to a second question was also important. The plaintiffs claimed that the current school funding system is failing to provide for the general diffusion of knowledge. This requires a determination of whether the current system of school finance provides enough funding to cover the costs of providing an adequate education for public school students in Texas. Because of the differences in the specification and estimation of the cost functions, the two studies generate different cost predictions; therefore, it is not surprising that they reach different conclusions about the adequacy of the current system. It is important to point out, however, that because the two studies made very different assumptions about the constraints imposed by the current system, even if they had used the exact same cost function and had identical predictions of costs, they would have reached different conclusions about the adequacy of current funding.

In their study, GJTB compared their predicted costs of meeting the 55% passing rate standard to the actual spending of each district. Only school districts with per-pupil expenditures less than predicted costs are considered to need additional funding. Any district that has spending equal to or greater than their predicted costs is assumed to have adequate funds to achieve the goals of the state's accountability system. This calculation assumes that if a district is currently spending more than it needs to spend to achieve the performance target, then it can reallocate its resources so as to meet the standard. Furthermore, by computing the tax rate, each district would need to raise revenue equal to the predicted level of spending and then conclude that "most West Orange-Cove Plaintiffs could lower their tax rates and still have enough revenue to cover their projected costs" (p. 11). Taylor (2004b) appeared to be arguing that if current spending is above the estimated costs of meeting the 55% passing rate standard, then this spending is not being used effectively and could be reduced or reallocated.

Taylor's (2004b) assessment of the adequacy of education funding in Texas was based on the premise that school districts have complete discretion to reallocate or eliminate all funding that is not directly associated with achieving the accountability standards included in the GJTB cost function analysis. For this premise to be justified, one must ignore the fact that the Texas accountability system includes a number of other requirements that are not included in the GJTB calculation of costs. These include requirements for proficiency in both science and social studies and requirements for raising graduation rates, stiffening grade promotion requirements, and reducing dropouts. In her testimony, Taylor (2004c, p. 179) argued that the costs of meeting these additional requirements and performance standards are included in the GJTB cost estimates, as long as those requirements and performance standards are highly correlated with the outcome measures included in the cost function. However, to the extent that reallocating funds toward efforts to increase math and reading scores reduces the ability of school districts to achieve these other requirements of the state's accountability system, the GJTB cost estimates underpredicted the cost of the accountability system as a whole. In addition to the accountability system, the state imposes a set of curriculum requirements on school districts, plus minimum class size requirements for the lower grades. These requirements further reduce the discretion of school districts in reallocating funds.

In their study, IR measured the additional costs of fulfilling the accountability standards by comparing their predicted cost of meeting the standards to the predicted cost of the district's current level of student performance. That is, the cost function results are used to calculate, for each school district, the predicted cost of the current passing rate. This amount is then subtracted from the predicted cost of meeting the 55% passing rate standard. This means that if a school district is already achieving the standard, they require no additional funding. Both the Texas accountability system and NCLB specify that in school districts where current student performance is substantially below the standards, districts are not required to meet the standard in a single year; rather, they must demonstrate AYP toward the standard. In calculating the additional cost of meeting the 55% passing rate standard, IR defined AYP as requiring school districts with current student performance below 52% to reach the standard over a 3-year period (i.e., moving one third of the way toward meeting the goal each year). Following this methodology, IR determined that the additional cost of meeting the 55% passing rate standard would be $1.7 billion (in 2004 dollars). This amount, which is equivalent to $405 per pupil, is equal to 6% of public school revenue in 2004.[15]

IR's additional cost calculations implicitly assumed that if school districts are currently spending more than what they need to spend to achieve their student performance goals, they are not able to reallocate current spending to meet the goal. This assumption is based on the premise that current spending is needed to meet accountability standards that are not included in the cost function estimates of additional costs, or to pay for needed resources that are not directly related to student performance measures. For example, many urban school districts may have little discretion over whether to spend money on security guards, and, perhaps especially in Texas, political realities may make it impossible to cut spending on school sports teams.[16]

---

[15]If all school districts were required to achieve a composite 55% passing rate standard on the reading and math exams in a single year, additional costs would be $5.4 billion.

[16]The recent film *Friday Night Lights* (Cameron, Whitaker, & Berg, 2004) illustrates the importance that high school football plays in many Texas communities.

The two studies take opposite views on the degree of discretion school districts have to eliminate or reallocate actual spending in excess of estimated costs. In drawing conclusions about whether public education in Texas is adequately funded, GJTB assumed that all spending in excess of estimated costs could be reallocated toward efforts to attain higher test scores. IR assumed that none of this excess spending is available for reallocation. These are both strong assumptions. Although we continue to believe that given state and federal mandates, contractual and other legal constraints, and political realities, most school districts have very little discretion in the reallocation of available funds; the true answer most likely lies somewhere in between the assumptions made by the GJTB and the IR studies.

The discussion so far has focused on a specific measure of educational adequacy, namely a 55% composite passing rate on the reading and mathematics exams. One issue raised by the plaintiffs in the *West Orange-Cove* case was whether this passing rate and the underlying cut scores (i.e., the number of correct answers needed to pass an exam) are sufficiently high to meet the constitution's general diffusion of knowledge requirement. Although the GJTB study estimated costs only for the 55% passing rate standard, IR provided additional cost estimates for several higher passing rate standards. Using the same procedures they followed in determining additional costs for the 55% rate standard, they calculated that additional costs (in 2004 dollars) would be $2.7 billion, $4.7 billion, and $10.1 billion to achieve the 60%, 70%, and 90% standards, respectively.

Primarily because of data limitations, both cost function studies almost certainly provide underestimates of the costs of meeting the accountability standards and provide an adequate education in Texas. Although the IR study discussed these shortcomings, the GJTB study did not. Three issues stand out. First, the cost calculations in both studies are based on a subset of the full array of accountability standards with which school district must comply. Not only do the TAKS accountability standards for 2005–06 include passing standards for social studies and science examinations, but there are new examination-linked standards for promotion from Grades 3, 5, 8, and a new 11th-grade examination that will be required for graduation. Second, although the accountability system requires that all the subgroups of students (White, Hispanic, African American, economically disadvantaged, and special education) within each school district must meet the academic standards, econometric problems forced the authors of both studies to assume that a school district met the standards if its overall passing rate exceeded the standard. Given that in many districts current student academic performance of economically disadvantaged, Black, and Hispanic students is substantially lower than their district's average performance, meeting the accountability standards separately for each subgroup of students will almost certainly require additional resources. Finally, the accountability system requires that school districts meet established passing rates in each subject. Both studies could only use passing rate data based on the average of the mathematics and the reading passing rates. It is again probable that additional resources beyond those calibrated in either study will be needed in districts where high reading passing rates mask low mathematics passing rates.

Lessons Learned

This article provides two examples of the use of econometric models in estimating the costs of meeting state education accountability standards. Despite the fact that the two econometric studies both involved the estimation of education cost functions and both provided estimates of the cost of meeting identical student performance standards in Texas, the authors of the two studies came to strikingly different conclusions. One study concluded that the current school funding system in Texas provides more than enough money to achieve the student performance goals set by the state's accountability system. The other study reached the conclusion that to meet the state's accountability standards, education spending would need to rise by several billion dollars. In this article, we spell out the various methodological choices made by the authors of both studies and, where possible, explain how these choices influenced both the econometric results and the policy conclusions that flowed from the results.

In discussing the strengths and weaknesses of the econometric approach to measuring educational adequacy, Baker et al. (2004) pointed out that "the underlying methodologies may rest on theoretical and analytical assumptions with which informed parties may disagree" (p. 20). Such disagreements are not uncommon in academic work. Academics often "agree to disagree" about their assumptions and leave the normative assessment of those assumptions to their readers. When the empirical findings of econometric analysis are used in judicial or legislative proceedings, however, it is particularly important that researchers both articulate and justify their assumptions and indicate how their assumptions affect their empirical results and policy recommendations. Policymakers and judges are much more likely to find the results convincing and credible if the underlying assumptions are sensible and are clearly articulated.

Among the lessons we take away from our experience in Texas is that to provide useful policy advice, it is important to make all assumptions clear and explicit and to discuss them fully. The plaintiffs in the *West Or-*

ange-Cove et al. v. Neeley et al. (2004) case adopted a strategy of highlighting the specification and estimation differences between the GJTB and IR studies, and noting how those differences affected the final conclusions about adequacy as we have done (albeit in more detail) in this article. It was a strategy that ultimately was persuasive to the court.

As Baker et al. (2004) also pointed out, it can be challenging to explain and communicate the assumptions, methodologies, and outcomes of econometrics methods such as educational cost functions. Guthrie and Rothstein (1999) criticized the use of cost function estimation, relative to professional judgment and successful schools approaches to estimating costs, because they believe that the cost function approach is too complex to explain to policymakers. The *West Orange-Cove* case demonstrates, however, that the courts *are* capable of understanding and using the results of complex statistical analysis. In his ruling, not only did Judge Dietz choose to rely on the IR cost function study rather than on the professional judgment study submitted by the plaintiffs, but his Findings of Fact (*West Orange-Cove et al. v. Neeley et al.*, 2004) specifically discussed many of the issues we have detailed in this article. For example, the judge questioned the decision of GJTB *not* to pupil weight, and he disagreed with their assumption regarding equivalent costs for improvement on the TAAS and TAKS exams.

At the same time, there is no question that econometric methods are generally less familiar to the courts and policymakers than more qualitative methods for estimating costs. Therefore, for those using econometric and other statistical techniques, it is important to choose a modeling strategy that is not overly complex. In conducting statistical analysis in a policy context, it is obviously important that the researcher be able to explain not only the results but also the methodological approach to an educated layperson.

It is also essential for researchers to recognize the limitations of whatever methodology they choose to employ. It is a mistake to "oversell" one's results. In the case of estimating the costs of providing an adequate education (or meeting any state accountability standard), it is important to recognize that no methodology has the ability to generate precise cost estimates.

The lawyers for the plaintiffs in the *West Orange-Cove* case understood this. They did not try to use the results of the IR study to argue that Texas would need to increase spending on education by a specific amount (e.g., nearly $2 billion to meet a 55% passing rate standard or about $5 billion to achieve a 70% standard). Rather, they used the IR study to provide evidence that the additional costs of meeting the standards exceeds, by a substantial amount, the money available for education funding under the current school funding system. In our view, none of the existing methodologies used to estimate the cost of meeting any educational standard is capable of providing precise cost estimates.

We conclude by underscoring our belief that econometric analysis has much to contribute to the measurement of educational costs. The *West Orange-Cove et al. v. Neeley et al.* (2004) case is the first time that cost functions have been used to assess adequacy in a judicial proceeding. We hope that it has demonstrated that although statistical methods may be more complicated than more qualitative approaches to estimating costs, they certainly need not be inaccessible. When presented carefully and with a full discussion of the limitations and underlying assumptions, econometric analysis can provide policymakers and the courts with a rigorous accounting of the costs of adequacy.

References

Alexander, C. D., Gronberg, T. J., Jansen, D. W., Keller, H., Taylor, L. L., & Treisman, P. U. (2000). *A study of uncontrollable variations in the costs of Texas public education* (Summary report for the 77th Texas Legislature). Austin: Charles A. Dana Center, University of Texas–Austin. Retrieved November 10, 2004, from http://www.utdanacenter.org/research/cei.php

Baker, B. D., Taylor, L., & Vedlitz, A. (2004). *Measuring educational adequacy in public schools* (Report prepared for the Texas Legislature Joint Committee on Public School Finance, The Texas School Finance Project). Retrieved October 25, 2004, from http://www.tlc.state.tx.us/roadmap/tsfp/Reports/Measuring%20Educational%20Adequacy.pdf

Cameron, J., Whitaker, J. (Executive Producers), & Berg, P. (Director). (2004). *Friday night lights* [Motion picture]. United States: Universal Pictures/Imagine.

Duncombe, W., Lukemeyer, A., & Yinger, J. (2004). *Education finance reform in New York: Calculating the cost of a "sound basic education" in New York City* (Policy Brief No. 28). New York: Syracuse University, Center for Policy Research, Maxwell School of Citizenship and Pubic Affairs.

Gronberg, T. J., Jansen, D. W., Taylor, L. L., & Booker, K. (2004). *School outcomes and school costs: The cost function approach* (Report prepared for the Texas Legislature Joint Committee on Public School Finance, The Texas School Finance Project). Retrieved October 25, 2004, from http://www.tlc.state.tx.us/roadmap/tsfp/Reports/school%20outcomes%20and%20school%20costs. doc2.pdf

Guthrie, J. W., & Rothstein, R. (1999). Enabling "adequacy" to achieve reality: Translating adequacy into state school finance distribution arrangements. In H. F. Ladd, R. Chalk, & J. Hansen (Eds.), *Equity and adequacy in education finance: Issues and perspectives* (pp. 209–259). Washington, DC: National Academy Press.

Imazeki, J., & Reschovsky, A. (2004a). *Estimating the costs of meeting Texas education accountability standards* (Report submitted to the plaintiffs as evidence in *West Orange-Cove et al. v. Neeley et al.*, District Court of Travis County, Texas, Rev. July 8).

Imazeki, J., & Reschovsky, A. (2004b). School finance reform in Texas: A never ending story? In J. Yinger (Ed.), *Helping children left behind: State aid and the pursuit of educational equity* (pp. 251–281). Cambridge, MA: MIT Press.

Murdock, S. H., White, S., Hoque, M. N., Pecotte, B., You, X., & Balkan, J. (2003). *The new Texas challenge: Population change and the future of Texas*. College Station, TX: A&M University Press.

National Center for Education Statistics. (2003). *Projections of education statistics to 2013, Section 1, Table 4: Enrollments in Grades K–12 in public elementary and secondary schools, by region and state, with projections: Fall 1994 to Fall 2013*. Washington, DC: Author.

No Child Left Behind Act of 2001, Pub. L. No. 107–110, 115 Stat. 1425 (2002).

Reschovsky, A., & Imazeki, J. (2003). Let no child be left behind: Determining the cost of improving student performance. *Public Finance Review, 31,* 263–290.

Smith, J. R., & Seder, R. C. (2004). *Estimating the cost of meeting state educational standards* (Report submitted to the plaintiffs as evidence in *West Orange-Cove et al. v. Neeley et al.*, District Court of Travis County, Texas). Davis, CA: Management Analysis & Planning, Inc.

Street, A. (2003). How much confidence should we place in efficiency estimates? *Health Economics, 12,* 895–907.

Taylor, L. L. (2000, April). The evidence on government competition. *Economic and Financial Review,* pp. 2–9. Available from http://www.dallasfedbackup.org/research/efr/2000/efr0002a.pdf

Taylor, L. L. (2004a). *Adjusting for geographic variations in teacher compensation: Updating the Texas Cost-of-Education Index* (Report prepared for the Texas Legislature Joint Committee on Public School Finance, The Texas School Finance Project). Retrieved November 1, 2004, from http://www.tlc.state.tx.us/roadmap/tsfp/Reports/Adjusting%20for%20Geographic%20Variations%20In%20Teacher%20Compensation.pdf

Taylor, L. L. (2004b). Estimating the cost of education in Texas (Report submitted to the state as evidence in *West Orange-Cove et al. v. Neeley et al.*, District Court of Travis County, Texas, Rev. July 26).

Taylor, L. L. (2004c). Trial testimony of Lori L. Taylor, September 8, 2004, *West Orange-Cove Consolidated Independent School District, et al. vs. Shirley Neeley, Texas Commissioner of Education, et al.* Travis County, Texas, 250th Judicial District, No. GV-100528.

West Orange-Cove Consolidated Independent School District, et al. vs. Shirley Neeley, Texas Commissioner of Education, et al. (2004). *Finding of Fact and conclusions of law* (Travis County, TX, 250th Judicial District, No. GV–100528, Presiding Judge John Dietz, November 30).

Exploring the Limits of Entitlement: Williams v. State of California

Thomas Timar
University of California, Davis

In August 2000, the American Civil Liberties Union filed a class-action lawsuit on behalf of school children against the state of California. The suit, *Williams v. State of California*, alleged that the state failed to exercise its constitutional obligation to provide equal access to education for all students in the state by allowing deficient facilities, uncredentialed teachers, and inadequate or insufficient instructional materials. A successful outcome for the plaintiffs would entail expansion of current boundaries of entitlement to a new standard that would establish constitutional entitlement to specific resources and a standard of state responsibility for oversight. In this article I examine whether the relief that plaintiffs seek pushes the definition of entitlement to areas beyond judicially manageable and constitutionally defensible standards.

The roles of lawyers, judges, and the courts in shaping American education policy has a history that dates to *Brown v. Board of Education* (1954). Advocates for various groups including women, racial and ethnic minorities, non-English speakers, children with handicaps and learning disabilities, among a host of others, have used the courts to challenge public policies and administrative practices that "reflect racist attitudes, repressive moralism, or bureaucratic callousness" (Kagan, 2001, p. 164). Among the most noteworthy changes in the system of education gover-

---

Requests for reprints should be sent to Thomas Timar, School of Education, One Shields Avenue, University of California, Davis, CA 95616. E-mail tbtimar@ucdavis.edu

nance over the past 40 years is legalization, defining education issues as legal issues to be resolved by lawyers and judges (Heubert, 1999; Kirp, 1988). Legal scholars also noted that although race lay at the base of the *Brown* decision, the justices' opinion went much beyond issues of race, "potentially enveloping within the judicial net all questions of equity in public schooling" (Kirp, 1986, p. 1). The principal objective of legalization was to secure basic universal education for all children and to achieve the large goal of educational equity by redefining concepts of educational entitlement.

Arguably, the most dramatic effect of legalization was the elaboration of procedural and substantive rights in just about all areas of education. *Goss v. Lopez* (1975), for instance, redefined the relationship between students and schools by effectively dismantling the concept of in loco parentis. *Tinker v. Des Moines* (1969) extended First Amendment rights to students with the court declaring that students do not shed their constitutional rights at the school house door. *Lau v. Nichols* (1974) required schools to " 'open the door to instruction' for students ... [with] linguistic deficiencies" (as cited in Yudof, Kirp, Levin, & Moran, 2002). The *PARC v. Commonwealth* (1971) and *Mills v. Board of Education* (1972) cases established a constitutional standard for education of disabled students. *Serrano v. Priest* (1971, 1974) in California established an equal protection standard for school finance.

In August 2000, the American Civil Liberties Union (ACLU)[1] filed a class-action lawsuit on behalf of school children against the state of California. The suit, *Williams v. State of California* (2000a), alleges that the state failed to honor its constitutional responsibility for providing equal access to education to all students in the state. According to plaintiffs, "there are too many schools in the State in which students face intolerably unequal conditions: pervasive over-crowding, absences of textbooks and trained teachers, and dismal and decaying school facilities" (p. 1). The suit charges that "in the face of repeated warning about shockingly poor school conditions and repeated calls for action, the State has failed to respond with remedies that are sufficient to cure the inequitable conditions" (p. 1). The legal basis for the case is that "the State holds a non-delegable constitutional duty to ensure that public school students in the State of California enjoy fundamentally equal educational opportunities" (*Williams v. State of California*, 2003, p. 3). According to plaintiffs,

---

[1]In addition to the ACLU, other firms joined the suit: Morrison Foerster LLP, the ACLU Foundation of Northern California, and Public Advocates Inc. The state of California retained the firm of O'Melvyny and Myers. The state also countersued school districts named in the suit.

the state has been derelict in performing that duty. Specifically, the suit charges that

> Tens of thousands of children attending public schools located throughout the State of California are being deprived of basic educational opportunities available to more privileged children attending the majority of the State's public schools. State law requires students to attend school. However, all too many California school children must go to schools that shock the conscience. Those schools lack the bare essentials required of a free and common school education that the majority of students throughout the State enjoy: trained teachers, necessary educational supplies, classrooms, even seats in classrooms, and facilities that meet basic health and safety standards. Students must therefore attempt to learn without books and sometimes without any teachers, and in schools that lack functioning heating or air conditioning systems, that lack sufficient numbers of functioning toilets, and that are infested with vermin, including rats, mice, and cockroaches. These appalling conditions in California public schools represent extreme departures from accepted educational standards and yet they have persisted for years and have worsened over time. Students who are forced to attend schools with these conditions are deprived of essential educational opportunities to learn. Plaintiffs bring this suit in an effort to ensure that their schools meet basic minimal educational norms. (*Williams v. State of California*, 2000a, p. 2)

The state's alleged dereliction of duty is alleged to be rooted in its system of oversight, which, according to the suit, has three major failings: (a) It fails to prevent unequal distribution of educational resources, (b) it fails to detect unequal distribution of resources, and (c) it fails to remedy unequal distribution of resources. The case focused on three areas of resource allocation: teachers, textbooks, and school facilities. Plaintiffs argued that there were systematic disparities in the distribution of these resources and that these disparities denied large numbers of students access to equal education. These failings and the harm they cause led plaintiffs to propose remedies, which they argued would improve the current system of state oversight and would eliminate the conditions that gave rise to the suit. Remedies were based on the creation of (a) statewide standards regarding teacher qualifications, facilities, and textbooks; (b) a system of monitoring districts and schools for adherence to state standards; and (c) a system of interventions and sanctions for schools and districts that are found noncompliant with state standards (*Williams v. State of California*, 2003, pp. 324–361).

Although *Williams* (2000a) had its legal antecedents in the *Serrano* (1974) and *Butt v. Honig* (1991) decisions, it is different from both traditional school finance equity cases and the "new wave"[2] of school finance adequacy cases in that it is not about the equity or adequacy of resources per se, but about the state's system of oversight for education—whether the state has a system of oversight that assures students adequate resources to benefit from the education provided them. According to the presiding judge, "this case will deal with the *management and oversight system* [italics added] that the state has in place to determine if they are legally adequate and whether they are being adequately implemented" (*Williams v. State of California,* 2000b, p. 3). Consequently, plaintiffs' proposed remedies in the case do not argue for reallocation or equalization of educational resources but for the creation of a state regulatory system that would ensure adequate resources to all students. A successful outcome in the case for plaintiffs would entail the expansion of current boundaries of entitlement to a new standard that would establish constitutional entitlement to specific resources and a standard of state responsibility for oversight.

The *Williams* (2000a) case raised important questions regarding the imposition of judicially manageable standards related to teacher qualifications, instructional materials, and facilities. In particular, the case raised questions about a process of adversarial legalism (Kagan, 2001) to produce better educational outcomes for students. In the history of school finance litigation, its principal goal has been to abolish unreasonable governmental barriers to equal opportunity. However, at what point do teacher qualifications, the quality and supply of instructional materials, and the conditions of school facilities deprive students of their constitutional entitlement to education? At what point are students denied access to education services because of these conditions? How might courts define a constitutionally defensible standard for a "good" teacher? Finally, are the proposed remedies likely to improve the state's system of oversight, or will they simply add to the complexity of the existing system of school oversight and governance? As I argue later, the suit—as much as it deals with the system of oversight and governance of the system of education—cannot be taken out of the political and policy contexts that shape the current system of education oversight and governance.

As much as the *Williams* (2000a) case was about the structure of state governance and oversight, I first examine the political and policy context of education in California and its impact on resource allocation—the factors that affect resource allocation related to teachers, instructional materi-

---

[2]See, generally, Heise (1995), Minorini and Sugarman (1999), and Verstegen and Knoeppel (1998).

als, and facilities. I then examine the remedies proposed by plaintiffs. Finally, I argue that proposed remedies are unnecessary and redundant and that redefining entitlement in terms of the state's obligation for oversight pushes the definition of entitlement to areas beyond judicially manageable and constitutionally defensible standards. Although one may agree with the normative goals for guaranteeing an adequate level of education for all students, turning normative goals into constitutional principles is a difficult undertaking. Redefining standards of educational equity and opportunity, as proposed by plaintiffs in the *Williams* case, are not likely to be realized through legalization but through political and administrative processes.

The Political and Policy Context for K–12 Education Oversight

Historically, responsibility for provision of education services in California, as in most states, has been broadly delegated to local school districts. In the State Constitutional Convention in 1879, the issue regarding public education that prompted the most prolonged debate was how specific the state constitution should be regarding education. After much debate, convention delegates voted to keep constitutional provisions sparse to the give the legislature flexibility to adjust the system to changing conditions as necessary. Delegates also realized that the state's size and variety required a system that could accommodate differences. Delegates eschewed a strong, centralized state role in the oversight of education in deference to a system of local decision making (*Debates and Proceedings*, 1880).

Created as legal entities, school districts were delegated authority to levy taxes, enter into contracts, and enforce state law as it applies to the operation of schools. Accountability for education was synonymous with political accountability. School board members answered to local electorates. If a community was unhappy with its schools, it could elect a new board, which then might replace the existing school superintendent. The scope and quality of educational services in a district was primarily determined by local preferences for education and the capacity to pay for them.

Although local districts were given broad authority to shape the basket of education goods in their communities (Tiebout, 1956), the state controlled districts through several means. The most basic of these were minimum standards, below which different kinds of school operations could not fall. Based on the rationale that "the general welfare requires a basic educational opportunity for all children" (*Serrano v. Priest*, 1971, 606; *Serrano II*, 1976), it justified requiring pupils to attend schools a minimum numbers of minutes each day for a minimum number of days per year as well as specifying what courses should be taught and what kind of training teachers needed to teach them (Policy Analysis for California Education, 1995). The state required districts to levy a certain level of tax and to pay its teachers a minimum salary.

However, a series of state policy actions, voter initiatives, and court decisions eroded the long-standing tradition of local control and dispersed authority among multiple agencies and levels of government. The cumulative impact of these events was twofold. It increasingly shifted decision making from local districts to the state, and it dispersed authority among an ever-growing number of players. *Centralization* of authority did not lead to *concentration* of authority. Rather than integrating authority, policymakers dispersed authority among various agencies. Currently, there are separate governing boards for the state university and community colleges. Teacher licensing and certification is under its own commission. For much of the time since Bill Honig's tenure as Superintendent of Public Instruction (SPI) during the 1980s, relations between the State Board of Education and the SPI have been highly contentious. As governors have come to compete with the SPI for control over public education, the power of the state board has risen at the expense of the superintendent's. During her tenure as state SPI, Delaine Eastin (1996) had little or no authority, was generally excluded from state-level policymaking, and was not regarded as a major force in state education politics or policy. The second effect of state policy activism has been the attenuation of local authority and diminution of local capacity to deliver educational services. Collective bargaining, the increasing share of categorical funding relative to block-grant funding, and increasing legislative directives to districts not only placed severe limitations on local discretion but also made local decision making vastly more complicated and expensive. Authority was not only dispersed at the local level but also among other actors such as the courts and the California Public Employees Relations Board.

The major policy impacts on school governance over the past 30 years are discussed next.

The Serrano v. Priest Decision

Historically, schools were supported primarily by local property taxes. Prior to 1979, state law set a base rate of property taxation to support public education. Voters in local districts could increase the rate if they wished to provide additional funding. However, large variations among communities in property wealth (measured by assessed valuation) meant that the amount of revenue raised for a given tax rate also varied considerably. As a result, low-wealth districts had to tax themselves at higher rates than wealthier districts to generate the same amount of revenue. The *Serrano* case challenged the constitutionality of the existing school finance system on equal protection grounds. The court agreed and directed the legislature to equalize funding among districts. The legislature's solution was Assembly Bill 65 in 1977. By means of complex equalization formulas, the measure intended to meet the *Serrano* mandate. However, the effects of AB 65 were superseded by Proposition 13.

Proposition 13

This constitutional amendment passed by voters in 1978 rolled back property taxes by 60%, limited the property tax rate to 1% of the assessed value, and held annual property tax increases to 2%. Any new taxes had to be approved by two thirds of the voters. (This last provision was modified in 2001 when the state's voters approved an initiative that reduced the required voting majority to 55% for local bond elections.) Its impact was to create a state school finance system. Combined with the limitations imposed on districts by *Serrano* (1974), district capacity to generate funds for education is now for all practical purposes nonexistent. Proposition 13 eroded local authority and capacity in several ways. It shifted leadership to the state. Both funding and policy decisions about education became the responsibility of the state. Local officials no longer turned to their local communities for support (and no longer did local communities hold local officials accountable for results), as most decisions shifted to Sacramento.

Proposition 98

Passed by voters in 1988, Proposition 98 assigned to K–12 and community colleges a constitutionally protected portion of the state budget by guaranteeing a minimum level of funding. The measure's intent was to provide stability and predictability in K–12 and community college funding from year to year. Although it has provided a guaranteed base, it has also become a ceiling for K–12 and community college funding. Perhaps its greatest impact, which is discussed more fully later, has been to use the state budget as a policy tool. Because policymakers do not know how much money will be available for the following year's budget, and because 40% of the money has to go to K–12 and community colleges, there is a last-minute scramble to spend money, as illustrated with the class-size reduction measure. Rather than putting the money into general revenues for schools, legislators increasingly targeted funds for special purposes. Although such decisions may have significant impacts on schools, there is little public discussion about them. The senate and assembly leadership of both parties, and the governor, generally make these decisions.

Collective Bargaining

The legislature authorized collective bargaining for school employees in 1976. Under previous provisions established by the Winton Act in 1965, districts were simply required to "meet and confer" with employee organizations. Collective bargaining greatly expanded teacher unions' rights to negotiate binding contracts with districts on a variety of matters. They include wages, hours, and other terms and conditions of employment such as employee benefits, teacher transfer policies, maximum class sizes, and evaluation procedures.[3] According to the California Commission for Educational Quality, California already had statutes in place regulating various employment-related matters such as state requirements for teacher tenure and dismissal, layoff notification, and maximum class size. These mandates were not eliminated when collective bargaining was enacted. Instead, existing statutes created a floor for the beginning of bargaining in districts. Moreover, the Rodda Act's (1975) original provisions relating to terms of employment and working conditions have been expanded through appeals processes and new laws so that its scope has expanded considerably. Collective bargaining contracts now typically cover a wide range of topics, most of which affect local capacity for service delivery. Collective bargaining rights related to compensation include cost-of-living adjustments, salary schedules, pay for specific duties, minimum teacher salaries, mentor teacher selection processes, tuition reimbursement, and travel expenses. Other areas covered by collective bargaining include benefits; hours and days of work; leaves; early retirement and retirement benefits; job assignment; evaluation procedures and remediation; grievance procedures, appeal processes, mediations, and arbitrations; discipline procedures and criteria; layoff and reemployment procedures; organization security; and a variety of other topics (EdSource, 1999).

According to Policy Analysis for California Education (PACE; 1995), "local teacher bargaining contracts centralized decision authority within districts, but also dispersed authority to legislatures, the courts, and public administrative agencies like the California Public Employee Relations Board" (p. 81). For districts, collective bargaining means that they *share* power with unions over a wide range of decisions that affect district educational policies and the distribution of district resources.

---

[3]See *California Government Code*, Article 4, § 3543–3543.8.

Categorical Funding

Traditionally, the principal forms of state subventions to schools was through unrestricted, block-grant funds. This meant that local boards had considerable discretion over the use of state funds. Over the past 15 years, and especially in the last 5 years, the legislature has shifted an increasingly larger share of state monies into categorical grants. These are restricted funds that may only be used for special purposes. In 1980, approximately 13% of all state subventions to school districts were restricted, and most of that was for three programs: special education, Title I, and Economic Impact Aid. In that year, there were also 19 categorically funded programs. Currently, there are roughly 124 categorically funded state programs, and such funds represent about 30% of per-pupil funding (Timar, 2004).

Increased reliance on categorical funding affects school districts in several specific ways. It has placed greater restrictions on districts regarding the use of state funds. It also means that as the share of categorical funding increases, education finance becomes increasingly supply driven: Expenditures are not necessarily driven by local needs but by the availability of funds. Categorical funding, moreover, usually comes with a list of programmatic and reporting requirements. Detailed proscriptions about parent advisory committees (many schools have four or five), reporting requirements, and fund expenditures have resulted in legislative micromanagement of districts.

More generally and more insidiously, the rise of categorical programs has balkanized schools and school districts. The proliferation of categorical funding has turned schools into collections of programs instead of coherent organizations. As the Coordinated Compliance Reviews conducted by the California Department of Education (CDE) show, schools and the state are mostly concerned with fairly narrow compliance issues while they may overlook the health of the organization as a whole. They also tend to encourage strict regulatory compliance over professional judgment and replace school goals with narrow programmatic goals (Kagan, 1986; Kirp & Jensen, 1986; Timar, 1994).

Federal Education Policy

Federal education policy amplifies the effects of state categorical funding. Most federal funds come with many regulations regarding their use, state which students are eligible to participate in federally funded programs, and under what conditions. No detail is too small to escape regulatory scrutiny. Schools, for example, were told that they could use federal Title I monies to carpet classroom floors if having students sitting on the floor was specifically called for in a teacher's lesson plans. They could not use federal funds for carpeting if students just happened to sit on the floor in the course of the day. Reauthorization of Title I in the fall of 2001—the No Child Left Behind Act—contained provisions that further invaded local decision making. States and schools are required to develop academic standards for all students and are required to test students. Low-performing schools that fail to show improvement over time may be "reconstituted"—teachers and principals may be replaced or, conceivably, the schools could be shut down. The law also requires states to certify that all teachers are "highly qualified."

Increased Legislative Activism

For the past 2 decades, the legislature has routinely enacted literally hundreds of measures dealing with K–12 education. However, the pace of legislative activity has intensified over the past 6 to 7 years. PACE (1995) noted that not only were initiatives of the past 7 years "unprecedented in terms of the consensus they represented among an otherwise divisive body" (p. 81), but also indicated an unusual level of intervention and top-down control by state-elected officials in the affairs of curriculum policy.[4]

Finding "the State"

Some analysts have described the 1990s as "a tumultuous decade for public education in California" (EdSource, 1999, p. 1). Over the course of the decade, teachers and local school officials have had to manage education programs while attempting to respond to an outpouring of new legislative initiatives. As analysts pointed out, the state has introduced numerous major new reforms and programs; some are aligned to larger goals, whereas others are not (p. 2). The major thrust of these reforms has been under the heading of "standards-based reform," most of which, although not all, have been introduced since 1995. The theory of standards-based reform is that the state adopts curriculum standards that, in turn, align with curriculum frameworks; student assessments; school accountability; and teacher training, professional development, compensation, and evaluation. The state is now on its third state assessment instrument in just over 10 years. The California Assessment Program (CAP), which had been in place since 1983, came to a halt in 1991 when Governor Deukmejian cut program funding just prior to leaving office. State policymakers re-

---

[4]California statute specifies that reading must be taught by means of phonics.

sponded by developing the California Learning Assessment System (CLAS) to replace it. Their goal was to create a state testing system that not only assessed individual student progress but was also based on the state's curriculum frameworks. CLAS proved to be short lived. A combination of conservative backlash to test content, negative research evaluations about the test's technical quality, and abysmally low scores on the first round of assessment resulted in Governor Wilson vetoing funding for CLAS. In 1996–97, districts were free to select their own tests. Policymakers soon realized, however, that it was difficult to compare student performance across schools and districts when schools used different tests. In 1997–98, the state adopted the Standardized Testing and Reporting Program, which used the Stanford 9 test. Over time, it has been augmented to measure state standards, which, although central to the state's education reform portfolio, were not assessed in the Stanford 9 (a nationally normed reference-based test). Stanford 9 has been replaced by the CAP6, which incorporates assessment of state standards.

Over the past 5 years, schools have been flooded with new programs and mandates. The state now bans social promotion and requires schools to provide remedial instruction for students during the summer. Students must pass a high school exit exam to receive a diploma, although implementation has been delayed due to the high rate of failure on the examination. The state Board of Education requires all students to take algebra in the 8th grade. These requirements come on top of class-size reductions, high-stakes accountability, and increasing restrictions in funding. At the same time, the demographic context of education is changing rapidly: The student population is becoming more diverse, many students are not proficient in English, and some districts face acute teacher and administrator shortages.

Although some individuals are critical of the substance of legislative initiatives, others are critical of the legislative process. Increasingly, major decisions about education are the products of last-minute deals made by a handful of people during budget negotiations. For instance, the Class Size Reduction Program enacted in 1996 to reduce class size in kindergarten and Grades 1 through 3 to not more than 20 pupils per teacher was introduced and passed into law in 1 day.[5] The statute appropriated $1.5 billion to school districts that participated in the program in the 1997–98 school year. It proved to be a politically popular measure. Schools liked it because it provided them $800 in per-pupil funding for participating grades. The

---

[5]SB 1777 (Chapter 163, *Statutes of 1996*). An earlier version of the same measure was contained in SB 1414, Greene. However, the latter became a measure to facilities to assist school districts with facilities-related costs associated with class-size reduction in K–3.

public and teachers liked it because it reduced class size from an average of 30 to 20. Class-size reduction also created a huge and sudden demand for teachers. Because many districts were already having difficulties in staffing classes with credentialed teachers, the measure exacerbated shortages for those districts. SPI, Delaine Eastin (1998), although an enthusiastic supporter of class-size reduction, tempered her enthusiasm with two concerns. One concerned the effectiveness of the $1.5 billion program if qualified teachers could not be found to staff those smaller classes. She estimated that the state might need over 18,000 new K–12 teachers at a time when there were already about 21,000 teachers with emergency credentials. She went on to state:

> Clearly, we would be alarmed if 21,000 doctors were working with emergency licenses, and we should be equally concerned about the training our teachers receive. Smaller classes are one important piece of the equation for a successful program, but skilled teachers are essential if we are to see real progress in student achievement based on challenging standards for all students. (Eastin, 1996)

The trajectory of education governance over the past 20 years has decidedly shifted toward the state and federal government. Increasingly, decisions traditionally left to local communities and school officials are now made at higher levels. Therefore, with inexorably increasing numbers of state players, it is difficult to know just who the "state" is or who in the state is responsible for the overall health of the state's education system. Categorical programs, collective bargaining, and a host of state and federal mandates have eroded local authority for resource allocation by shifting authority to more distant reaches of government. Therefore, although state oversight has become increasingly dispersed as the educational policy sphere has become more complex, local officials have much less discretion about the delivery of instructional services and the resources necessary to provide them.

School Finance and Control of Resource Allocation

Changes in state and local governance are perhaps most dramatically exemplified in the financing of schools. Until the late 1970s, local property tax revenues comprised the major share of school funding. The state's role in direct fiscal support to schools was a limited one. It guaranteed a funding floor for districts (as long as districts taxed themselves at a state-specified minimum level) and provided additional dollars for extraordinary costs (e.g., for transportation in rural areas). In 1969–70, local property taxes provided, on average, 60% of K–12 funding, whereas the state provided 34%. Federal dollars made up the remaining 6%. Most important, nearly 90% were general purpose or unrestricted, which meant that districts had a free hand in deciding how to allocate revenues.

The present school finance system is radically different. On average, schools receive 60% of their funding from the state, 28% from local sources, 10% from the federal government, and 2% from the state lottery. Moreover, of the 60% that comes from the state, 40% is restricted; this means that money must be used only for state-specified purposes. How much money a school district receives is fixed in law. Although districts do have authority to augment their revenues through parcel taxes, only a handful have succeeded in doing so. For all practical purposes, California has a state-financed education system.

In the post–Proposition 13 school finance system, a district's revenues are determined not by local fiscal capacity or local preference but by the state legislature. How much schools have to spend and, increasingly, how they spend it is determined at the state (not the local) level and is dependent on a variety of factors. Among them are state fiscal capacity, statewide voter preferences for education spending, and the degree to which education can compete with other funding sectors. As school finance decision making shifts to the state arena, it engages new actors—legislators and politically mobilized interests with access to them. Reflecting the new politics of school finance in California is the inexorable expansion of categorical or restricted funding—in quantity and as a share of total funding. Increasingly, decisions about local expenditures—how much to spend on textbooks, staff development, or instructional materials, for instance—are made at the state level.

The most dramatic change in the state's school finance system has been in the growth of categorical (restricted) funding. In 1980, there were 19 state and federal categorically funded education programs in California. By 2002, there were 124. Moreover, in 1980–81 about 13% of funding was restricted, most of it going for special education costs. The remaining 87% of funding was unrestricted, to be spent at the discretion of districts. In 2000–01, nearly 33% of school funding was restricted. Roughly 40% of state money to schools is in the form of categorical funding. Between 1980 and 2000, average per-pupil funding increased by 15% (in Year 2000 constant dollars), from $5,422 to $6,232. Over that period, the restricted share of those dollars increased from $705 to $1,870 (a 165% increase), whereas unrestricted share declined by nearly 8%, from $4,717 to $4,362. For a class of 30 students, that represents a decline in discretionary spending of $10,650. If the share of restricted to nonrestricted funding had remained the same in

2000 as it was in 1980, it would amount to nearly $32,000 per class of 30 students.

In California, only a handful of districts have the capacity to generate significant local revenues. Some districts, about 16, have succeeded in passing parcel taxes to support schools. Other districts, approximately 64, are so-called basic aid districts, which means that they exceed their state-imposed revenue limits. For the remaining 900 or so districts in the state, their revenues are determined by the annual state budget. The combined lack of local capacity to generate additional revenues and the increasingly prescriptive nature of state funding, schools have little control over spending. In addition, salaries and benefits compose, on average, 84% of district expenditures.

Since Proposition 13, the state has had to compensate for the decline in property tax revenues. Consequently, K–12 funding now competes with other state and local government activities: transportation, health and welfare, safety, higher education, natural resources, energy, and a host of others. Although it is true that California has slipped from its once preeminent position as national leader in school funding, given the fact that education finance is now a zero-sum game, K–12 has managed to hang on to its share of funding. As noted earlier, per-pupil funding in California increased by 15% in constant dollars. Over the same period, teacher salaries increased 25% in constant dollars, whereas median family income rose 16%.

The increase in overall funding is reflected in changes in specific funding areas. Professional development is an area of funding that has grown significantly over the past 20 years. Between 1983 and 1986, it grew from $3 million annually to over $100 million. Between 1997–98 and 2001, funding to the University of California for K–12 staff development increased from $32 million to over $230 million. In 2001–02, the state budget for K–12 included $514 million for various staff development programs. This figure does not include the funding available for staff development that is embedded in various school accountability provisions that total to just under $2 billion.

Senate Bill 813 in 1983–84 provided, for the first time, an annual apportionment of $14.41 ($26.25 in Year 2000 dollars) per pupil in Grades 9 through 12 for purchase of instructional materials. Legislation specifically required that these funds be used by districts to supplement, not supplant, instructional materials purchases. Previously, state funding for textbook purchases was provided only for pupils in Grades K–8, at a statutory rate of $21.18 ($37.70 in Year 2000 dollars) per pupil. High schools had funded instructional materials out of their regular apportionments. For the 2000–01 school year, the apportionment was $36 per elementary student and $13 per high school student. In constant dollars, funding for instructional materials over the period declined by 4.5% for elementary students and by 50% for high school students. It is important to note, however, direct state support for instructional materials and supplies pays for only a fraction of actual school expenditures. For 2000–01, average expenditures by schools for textbooks ($83), other instructional textbooks ($33), instructional materials ($127), and other supplies ($105) totaled to $348 per pupil (Legislative Analyst, 1984).

The data suggest that over a 20-year period current funding for K–12 education increased in real terms. However, that increase was mostly absorbed by teacher costs—salaries and professional development.

In addition to increasing current funding, the state has also increased funding for school facilities construction and modernization. Between 1990 and 2000, voters approved $15.8 billion in new construction and modernization bonds for K–12 education. Assembly Bill 16 in 2002 authorized a $10 billion state bond measure that voters approved in March 2004. The measure adds $5.26 billion for new facilities construction, $2.25 billion for modernization, and $2.44 billion for the 2004 Critically Overcrowded Schools Facilities Account. With passage of the latest bond measure, the state will have authorized nearly $26 billion in funding for construction and renovation. In 2000, voters approved Proposition 39, which lowered the voter approval requirement for local bond elections to 55%. This means that the local match that is required to apply for state funds will be easier for districts to meet. It also means that the $10 billion in proposed funding would be matched by another $10 billion of local funding. Given the state and local investment in capital outlay and renovation, it is difficult to conclude that the state is not making a concerted effort to provide funding to add new facilities and improve existing facilities.

The Importance of Policy Continuity and Stability

Plaintiffs in the *Williams* (2003) case pointed to North Carolina and Connecticut as states that have engineered significant changes in student achievement across all socioeconomic status (SES) groups (p. 334). They argued that both states made major investments in education chiefly by increasing teacher salaries, funding professional development, and improving preservice training of teachers. As a result, "North Carolina has posted the largest student achievement gains in mathematics and reading of any state in the nation " (p. 334). Connecticut, similarly, has also "made significant progress, becoming the highest achieving state in the nation, despite and increase in the proportion of low-income and limited-English proficient students during that time" (p. 334).

A study in 1998 by RAND researchers for the National Education Goals Panel entitled, *Exploring Rapid Achievement Gains in North Carolina and Texas,* came to very different conclusions regarding the reasons for high levels of achievement. According to that study, Texas and North Carolina made greater combined student achievement gains in math and reading on the National Assessment in Educational Progress in 1992–1996 than any other states. According to the study, these gains were "significant and sustained." In addition, the two states "made significant improvement on more measures of progress toward National Education Goals than any other states" (Grissmer & Flannagan, 1998, p. iii). In the study's preface, the researchers state that achievement gains were found *not*[6] to be due to increased real per-pupil spending, reduced teacher–pupil ratios (class size), or having more teachers with advanced degrees or more years of experience. Researchers attribute achievement growth to leadership from the business community, political leadership, and continuity and stability of reform policies over time. Finally, the key school reform strategies were statewide academic standards, holding all students to the same standards, statewide assessments closely linked to academic standards, accountability systems with consequences for results, increased local flexibility for administrators and teachers, systems and data for monitoring improvement, shifting resources to schools with more disadvantaged students, and an infrastructure to sustain reform (Grissmer & Flannagan, 1998, p. ii).

A study of mathematics and science reform in eight states conducted for the National Science Foundation in 1996 drew similar conclusions regarding the characteristics of successful school reform efforts[7] (Timar, Kirst, & Kirp, 1995). The study found that Connecticut had, indeed, made considerable gains in student achievement—more than the other states in the study. And, most important, researchers attributed Connecticut's success to strong and consistent policy leadership, the autonomy of the state education agency to develop and sustain a long-term reform plan, the lack of legislative interference, the continuity and stability of reform policies over time, and statewide assessments that were closely aligned with standards. As plaintiffs pointed out, Connecticut also had a massive infusion of funds for teacher salaries. As a result, teacher salaries in Connecticut consistently rank among the top five in the nation (after cost-of-living adjustments), often alternating with California for first- or second-highest teacher salaries in the nation.

State strategies to improve schools in California are similar to the strategies of other states. Reform policies have targeted professional develop-

---

[6]This emphasis was in the original.
[7]Study conducted under a grant from the National Science Foundation.

ment, higher salaries, preservice and credentialing, and state standards and assessments. A striking difference between California and other states is the instability of the policy environment in which education operates. As described earlier, there is little stability, continuity, or consistent leadership. The state has adopted and rejected at least three assessment instruments. New programs are enacted with little time for schools to prepare for their implementation. The legislature increasingly micromanages schools from Sacramento. Schools and districts have virtually no flexibility for resource allocation. Those critical ingredients for success that have characterized states like Connecticut and North Carolina are sorely missing from California.

Revenue and Expenditure Patterns Among Districts

If one compares expenditures and funding in low-performance districts to the state average and to high-performing schools, it is not readily apparent what accounts for variability among schools and districts in instructional materials, facilities, and teacher experiences. Table 1 displays differences in district expenditures and total revenue sources for what can be termed *high-need* districts, *low-need* districts, and the average of all districts.[8]

The table shows differences in expenditures and revenues among average, high-need and low-performing, and low-need and high-performing districts. Students in high-need districts receive over $100 more per pupil in total revenues than the state average and just under $500 more than the low-need districts. However, although low-performing district spending on certificated employees is close to the state average, high-performing district spending is slightly more than $300 per pupil higher. High-performing districts also spend almost $100 less per pupil than the state average and $200 less than low-performing districts.

Plaintiffs argued that states that have shown the highest improvement for all, including low-SES students, have targeted additional state funds to

---

[8]High need is defined as those districts (often cited by plaintiffs) that are in the bottom quartile of performance based on the average Academic Performance Index (API), in the top quartile of percentage of teachers with emergency credentials, and in the bottom quartile of SES. Low need is top quartile of API, bottom quartile of percentage of teachers with emergency credentials, and top quartile of SES. (Data are for 2001–02.) The SES or "need" index combines several district indicators: the percentage of African American and Hispanic students, the percentage of English learners, the percentage of students whose parents qualify for CalWorks, the percentage of students eligible for free or reduced price lunch, and average parent education level. These variables are scaled, added, and weighted to give more significance to the combination of all variables.

Table 1

Comparison of Revenues and Expenditures by High-Need/Low-Performing and by Low-Need/High-Performing Districts

Variable	State Average	High Need	Low Need
Revenues			
Per-pupil total revenues	$7,823	$7,959	$7,465
Categorical funds	$1,556	$1,864	$1,298
State revenue limit	$5,129	$4,803	$4,891
Expenditures			
Capital outlay	$176	$199	$114
Services	$868	$890	$847
Books and supplies	$476	$568	$359
Benefits	$1,130	$1,137	$996
Classified salaries	$1,224	$1,211	$1,084
Certificated salaries	$3,466	$3,417	$3,763

Note. High need is defined as those districts (often cited by plaintiffs) that are in the bottom quartile of performance based on average Academic Performance Index, in the top quartile of percentage of teachers with emergency credentials, and in the bottom quartile of socioeconomic status (SES). Low need is top quartile of Academic Performance Index, bottom quartile of percentage of teachers with emergency credentials, and top quartile of SES. (Data are for 2001–02). The SES, or Need, index combines several district indicators: the percentage of African American and Hispanic students, the percentage of English learners, the percentage of students whose parents qualify for CalWorks, the percentage of students eligible for free or reduced lunch, and average parent education level. These variables are scaled, added, and weighted to give more significance to the combination of all variables.

low-SES, low-performing districts. The data in Table 1 show a strong redistributive effect for state revenues. As noted, total per-pupil revenues in low-SES, low-performing districts receive, on average, slightly $100 above the state average but over $400 above high-SES, high-performing districts. High-need districts receive $566 more in categorical funds than low-need districts. On average, districts' revenue limits are $2,924 local revenue and $2,606 state apportionments. For high-need districts, the comparable figures are $1,509 and $3,404, whereas for low-need districts, comparable figures are $3,574 and $1,253. Taken together, high-need, low-performing schools receive, on average, just over $3,000 more in state revenues than low-need, high performing districts. Based on these data, it is difficult to conclude that California has not made a substantial financial effort to aid high-need districts.[9]

---

[9]It is arguable whether school funding is adequate in absolute terms; the data show that high-need schools are not disadvantaged with respect to state support in comparison to average and low-need schools.

Will Plaintiffs' Remedies Result in Higher Achievement for Low-Income Students in Low-Performing Schools?

Plaintiffs argued that an oversight system comprised of standards, compliance monitoring, and interventions and sanctions regarding instructional materials, qualified teachers, and facilities is essential and will, in fact, create a more equitable system of education. This system of oversight, moreover, would be modeled on the Fiscal Crisis Management Assistance Team concept, which was created by AB 1200 (California State Assembly Bill 1200) in the wake of Richmond Unified School District's fiscal collapse. In the following section I examine those proposed remedies.

Standards Regarding Instructional Materials

Although it is reasonable and desirable that each child shall have a textbook that is in good condition, reasonably current, and available for a student to complete homework, the reasons why some students do not have access to such books are not well documented. There are cases of teachers not using new textbooks because they prefer the older ones, ones on which they have built lesson plans. Books are also destroyed and mutilated. In some instances, it may be that schools have deferred purchasing textbooks while waiting to implement new standards; in other instances, schools may have deferred because they have other short-term funding priorities. Elk Grove Unified School District, for example, estimates that adoption of a new language arts series for the district cost approximately $7 million with an additional $2 to $2.5 million for professional development costs associated with the adoption. As Table 1 shows, the reasons do not appear to be related to expenditures, as low-performing districts spend nearly $100 per pupil more than the state average and about $200 more than high-performing districts.

As plaintiffs noted, the Education Code already regulates textbooks and instructional materials. California Education Code Sections 60117–60119, (a) 1 state

> The governing board shall hold a public hearing or hearings at which the governing board shall encourage participation by parents, teachers, members of the community interested in the affairs of the school district, and bargaining unit leaders, and shall make a determination, through a resolution, as to whether each pupil in each school in the district has, or will have prior to the end of that fiscal year, sufficient textbooks or instructional materials, or both, in each subject that are consis-

tent with the content and cycles of the curriculum framework adopted by the state board.

State law further requires districts to take specific remedial actions if it is determined that there are insufficient textbooks and materials. Plaintiffs' remedies would simply duplicate existing law.

Standards Regarding Qualified Teachers

Plaintiffs' standards regarding qualified teachers would require that at least 80% of teachers at each school and at least 80% of teachers on each track with multitrack programs be fully credentialed and that those teaching English language learners be specially authorized to teach them. In addition, low-performing schools should be prohibited from having more than the state average proportion of teachers without preliminary or clear credentials.

The remedy raises several questions. First among them is why 80%? Is there something particularly compelling about that percentage of credentialed teachers? Is it based on some measure of school effectiveness? The 80% requirement is problematic also because federal law, No Child Left Behind (2001), requires *all* teachers to be fully credentialed and certified in their subject areas. California's State Board of Education has developed a plan for implementation of the federal law by 2005–06 (California Department of Education, 2004).

The second question regards existing capacity to meet the requirement. For schools to meet the 80% requirement, 442 schools in 62 districts would have to hire approximately 4,500 teachers. To meet the state average requirement—9.5% in 2001–02—1,710 schools in 122 districts would have to find approximately 13,000 teachers.[10] It is difficult to imagine where those teachers could be found. Most likely, many would come from the existing pool of teachers with emergency credentials who are simultaneously enrolled in teacher credentialing programs.

A further problem with plaintiffs' remedies is that they are based on several questionable assumptions. One is that all teachers with emergency credentials are unqualified to teach, whereas those on full credentials are qualified. The assumption is that the latter are better, more effective teachers than the former. There is little evidence to support the assumption that credentialing alone equates with competence. Private and parochial

---

[10]These calculations are based on a composite data set created by Thomas Timar. The data set includes data from the California Department of Education's (2001–02) J200, J300, Academic Performance Index data files, and demographic data files.

schools do not require credentials. However, teachers in those schools are generally thought to be quite competent. If one were to take a competent, uncredentialed teacher out of, say, Jesuit High School in Sacramento, California, and place him into Sacramento High School, would that teacher suddenly become incompetent? What should we think about the competence of credentialed, experienced teachers who hate their jobs, are indifferent toward their students, and are just hanging on until they retire? What about those credentialed teachers who have long ago given up on teaching and are just there to babysit students?

The efficacy of plaintiffs' remedies is further undermined by the fact that they focus only on the symptoms of problems while they ignore their underlying causes. Teacher seniority provisions in collective bargaining contracts, for example, are one reason that low-performing schools have a larger percentage of inexperienced teachers. Schools and districts are not free to assign teachers based on instructional need, but assign based on seniority. Teachers with high seniority—the most experienced—flee to high-SES, high-performing schools. As noted earlier, the state's class-size reduction measure created a huge demand for teachers. Consequently, the best teachers went to schools that offered more attractive working conditions. In this instance, the unpredictability of the policy and political environment was responsible for flooding the state with teachers with emergency credentials. It is hard to imagine how plaintiffs' remedies would create greater predictability in the system.

Plaintiffs argue that districts with high percentages of teachers with emergency credentials should do more to attract credentialed, experienced teachers. However, it is doubtful that the teachers' union would agree to a dual salary schedule that rewarded teachers who teach in low-performing, low-SES schools.

There is little disagreement regarding the goal of having qualified, good teachers in every classroom. However, it is doubtful that plaintiffs' remedies would achieve that objective. They cite court actions in other states as examples of court-mandated reforms. However, little is known about the efficacy of those reforms. Requiring, as the court did in North Carolina, that schools be staffed by "caring" teachers and principals is one thing. Developing a legally defensible standard for caring and proposing to hold teachers and principals accountable to that standard is quite another.

Remedies Regarding Facility Standards, Compliance Monitoring, and Enforcement

It is reasonable to expect that schools should adhere to state standards for safety and cleanliness. Reasonable people would agree that schools should be safe, clean, uncrowded, and generally well maintained. The general attainment of these standards depends on the ability of districts to build new facilities, modernize existing ones, and provide routine maintenance. As in other areas, plaintiffs are silent as to why some districts have not built new schools to alleviate overcrowding, why others have not renovated or upgraded existing facilities, and why in some districts routine facilities maintenance is allowed to lapse. Schools might not be built because districts were not able to raise local matching funds through local bond elections as long as they needed two-thirds voter approval for passage. As noted earlier, state voters have quite consistently (with one exception) approved school facilities bonds. The March 2004 bond election provided $2.4 billion to critically overcrowded schools. How much schools spend on maintenance is determined by competition for a fixed amount of resources. As noted earlier, discretionary funds to districts are less, in constant dollars, than they were 20 years ago. Because personnel costs comprise on average just over 80% of district expenditures, there is little maneuvering room for districts. How likely would it be that teachers would agree to freeze their salaries for 5 years, for instance, so a district could undertake maintenance and renovation projects?

In this instance also, plaintiffs ignore the underlying causes for overcrowding and deterioration of facilities. As noted earlier, class-size reduction created a huge demand not only for teachers but also for classrooms. Districts needed to find classrooms for 18,000 new teachers. Although class-size reduction had an accompanying measure to fund temporary school facilities, the major problem faced by many districts was finding room to locate them. Districts like Los Angeles were faced with the choice of building over playgrounds, resorting to a year-round schedule, or busing students over long distances. Moreover, construction of new facilities is a long, complicated process that involves many steps—land acquisition (often through condemnation proceedings), permit requests, and environmental impact studies to name just a few—that can be challenged and delayed. Districts must also contend with the often-present "not in my backyard" factor. Communities may want to relieve crowding by building new schools so long as the schools are not built in their neighborhoods.

Plaintiffs' remedies would create a new regulatory bureaucracy whose job it would be to promulgate regulations (obviously state standards will require interpretation and in cases of dispute mediation), monitor for compliance, and impose interventions. Some of the new responsibilities would be assigned to the CDE and others to county superintendents. Given that the operating budget of the CDE has been drastically reduced to the point where nearly 80% of its operating budget comes from federal sources, there is no reason to think that there is much organizational slack to take on new monitoring responsibilities. It is also worth noting that county superintendents already are empowered by the state constitution to "superintend" the schools within their counties. That means, presumably, that superintendents or their designees could visit schools on a regular basis and write reports on conditions of schools. Those could be available to both state officials and the public. Although this would be costly, it might be less burdensome than plaintiffs' requiring that all schools send reports to the state regarding the status of their facilities. One wonders who would read over 9,000 reports. Moreover, would such reports be required once a year? If so, might that encourage Potemkin Village behavior? Would they be required quarterly, in which case there would be over 36,000 reports to read? And what would monitors do about checking the accuracy of the school reports? Would they visit schools to see if windows and bathrooms are clean and drinking fountains are in good repair? Of course, this sort of compliance monitoring says nothing about what schools should do in cases where students vandalize bathrooms and drinking fountains, spray graffiti on walls, or break windows.

Although monitoring would be costly, interventions would be difficult, redundant, and more costly. For instance, plaintiffs would have the state establish yet another bureaucracy by having state monitors "help districts assess for eligibility for bond funding, timely file their applications, and take appropriate steps to raise local matching funds, or justify their hardship applications" (*Williams*, 2002, p. 353). This seems to ignore the fact that there are already consulting firms who work with districts in each phase of the facility's construction or modernization process. Because they seem to be quite good at it, why not continue to rely on them? Why use limited state resources to establish a state bureaucracy when an efficient process already exists?

Finally, remedies would have an external entity to require and oversee local bond applications in the event that districts do not initiate them on their own; there is some state determination that the district should, indeed, apply for funds. Because the state, except in cases of hardship, requires a 50–50 match, one assumes that the monitoring entity will also run the local bond election campaign, presumably regardless of whether voters wanted it or not. Given the difficulty of mounting a successful bond campaign, it is unlikely that such an effort could be successful. Then, plaintiffs would have monitors remain for the duration of the facility' project to "ensure that the capital construction projects are properly managed, work is completed according to schedule, and funds are not wasted" (*Williams*, 2002, p. 354). Would such monitors replace, supersede, or work alongside community oversight committees established by Proposition 39, the Strict Accountability in Local School Construction Bonds Act of 2000, and

Section 15264 *et seq.* of the Education Code, to oversee facility construction projects?

Plaintiffs' Remedial Model and the Problem of Entitlement

The underlying argument in the *Williams* (2000a) case is that the state is derelict in its constitutional obligation to oversee schools; responsible for ensuring that they have adequate numbers of qualified teachers; responsible for sufficient and adequate instructional materials; and responsible for clean, well-maintained, uncrowded facilities. This suggests, furthermore, that there are systematic; pervasive; and, over time, predictable barriers that deprive students of their constitutional entitlement to equal education. The suit assumes, first, that it is possible to construct legally defensible standards for schools regarding facilities, teachers, and facilities; second, that the state system of oversight it proposes will ensure that those standards are met; and, third, that implementation of those standards will guarantee all students with adequate educational resources.

Plaintiffs' efforts to extend entitlement to a set of principles and policies for state oversight of education run into the problem of how to render normative arguments based on understandings of distributive justice into claims of a constitutional nature. Although we may agree with the normative arguments, constructing legally imposed remedial interventions is an entirely different proposition. As an example of institutional reform litigation, the *Williams* (2000a) case sought to satisfy plaintiffs' aspirations to equality, opportunity, and fair treatment—the legalization agenda in education for the past 50 years. The question is whether the courts are suited to fashion the remedy to satisfy those aspirations. There is a real demarcation between problem solving generally and legal problem solving. The standard that plaintiffs sought points to issues of educational quality and excellence rather than equalization of resources. Whether those standards can be achieved through a process of adversarial legalism is questionable. The issues in the case have more to do with the quality of instruction than equalization of educational resources. Would it matter what kind of credentials teachers had if students in schools with uncredentialed teachers were scoring in the top quintile on the API? Conversely, if mostly African American students in brand new facilities stocked with ample instructional materials, taught by fully credentialed teachers in a district that spent $10,000 more per pupil than the average district in the state, were scoring in the bottom quartile of the API, would plaintiffs be satisfied? Would the education to which those students are entitled be met? The tension between policy aspirations and constitutionally protected rights is a core tension in the *Williams* case. Aspirations to high-quality education for all students, regardless of race, ethnicity, or wealth, are not expressed in the language of civil rights—the language of duty and obligations—but in the language of effective schools. They are framed in terms of what Fuller (1964) called the "morality of aspirations." Aspirations go beyond regulation as "there is no way that law can compel a man to live up to the excellences of which he is capable" (p. 9). For that reason, the kinds of educational outcomes that the plaintiffs sought cannot rely on rules and mandates, as accounting procedures, reporting requirements, and compliance monitoring have little to do with attaining those ends.

Another tension inherent in the case is that of remedying violations as opposed to defining constitutional rights. If the plaintiffs' objective was to remedy what they believed were violations of law, it would seem logical and appropriate to pursue appropriate administrative and political remedies. However, plaintiffs did not pursue administrative remedies. Instead, plaintiffs argued that the court should extend the state's constitutional right to education to embrace some level of teacher qualifications, instructional materials, and facilities. Because the alleged violations are contextual, conditional, and temporary, and not based in legal obstacles, it is difficult to know just what those rights might be and how they could be judicially monitored and enforced. As noted earlier in the discussion, there are simply too many factors that determine the quality of education service delivery to allow the courts to fashion a single standard that could be uniformly applied.

The state requires schools and districts to report a vast amount of data. According to a study undertaken in the mid-1980s, the state required districts and schools to submit over 87 reports in a 6-month period (Bardach, 1986). The School Report Card requires a mind-numbing amount of data from schools. Most of the data, moreover, must cover a 3-year period. One wonders how districts can reasonably obtain some of the required data and what policymakers will do with it once they get it. For instance, schools must report on the availability of substitutes in the community. As plaintiffs pointed out, many of the reports submitted by schools are pro forma: all schools in a given district will submit essentially the same report. As a result, the school report cards are meaningless, providing policymakers, parents, and the community no usable information. However, this points to the chief weakness of regulatory bureaucracies of the kind proposed by the plaintiffs. They tend to lapse into formalism and legalism as attention shifts from school improvement to regulatory compliance. The penchant for formalism displacing school improvement goals is well documented (see Kirp & Jensen, 1986). A rough cost–benefit analysis suggests that the direct and indirect costs to the state, counties, and districts of creating a new regulatory bureaucracy are high, whereas benefits are few.

The fact is that districts are responsive to deficiencies in the system. However, deficiencies may not be easily remedied in the short run. Because of voter approved state facilities bonds, the state provides funding for new construction and renovation. Teachers who now teach with emergency credentials are enrolled in teacher credentialing programs and within 1 or 2 years will have full credentials. Problems regarding teachers, instructional materials, and facilities that plaintiffs described are not static and do not exist in a static policy environment. It makes little sense then to create a massive and costly regulatory bureaucracy when many of the problems that plaintiffs pointed to may be significantly ameliorated and, in many cases, totally eliminated.

Conclusion

There are numerous tensions in a system of education governance, tensions that policymakers and social reformers must balance. What is wanted, according to one scholar, is nothing less than a decision-making mode that is

> at once responsive to national concerns and local variability; attentive to professional perceptions and political preferences; sensitive to the rights of the worst-off, yet resistant to the rigidities that accompany the degeneration of legality into legalism; and able to foster both compliance to rule and organizational adaptability. (Kirp, 1986, p. 14)

Although legal strategies for institutional reform have served as a vital mechanism for raising issues of social justice that are ignored by elected branches or public officials, there is the danger that it lapses into rigidities and legalism and displaces the attainment of educational objectives with regulatory and legal compliance. In an environment where social policy aspirations are difficult to attain, it is often too easy to substitute numbers of credentialed teachers, square feet of space per student, numbers of bathrooms, and numbers of textbooks and computers for education quality.

In a recent study of law and school reform, Heubert (1999) underscored concerns regarding the capacity of legalization to improve educational quality. Heubert noted that

> the growing convergence of legal standards and educational norms—which reflects a recognition that legal remedies for educational prob-

lems are likeliest to succeed if they take educational considerations properly into account—affects virtually every law-based school reform effort, and will influence the roles that lawyers, educators, researchers, parents and courts play in the reform process. (p. 32)

Such caveats are particularly applicable in the *Williams* (2000a) case as plaintiff attorneys attempted to expand educational entitlement to embrace the governance and oversight of education. There is little doubt that lawyers and courts will continue to play an important role in education policymaking. Whether law-driven reforms will improve schools is less certain if such remedies are pursued only through the courts.

References

Bardach, E. (1986). Education paperwork. In D. Kirp & D. Jensen (Eds.), *School days, rule days* (pp. 124–145) Philadelphia: Falmer.

Brown v. Board of Education, 347 U.S. 483, 74 S.Ct. 686, 98 L.Ed. 873 (1954).

Butt v. Honig, 4 Cal. 4th 685 (Cal. 1991).

California Department of Education. (2004). *NCLB teacher requirements resource guide*. Retrieved December 6, 2004, from http://www.cde.ca.gov/nclb/sr/tq/nclbnewfaq.asp

California Education Code, Sections 60117–60119, (a) 1.

California Government Code, Article 4, § 3543–3543.8

California State Legislature. (1991). Chapter 1213, *Statutes of 1991*. Sacramento, CA: California State Printing Office.

California State Legislature (1996). Chapter 163, *Statutes of 1996*. Sacramento, CA: California State Printing Office.

California State Legislature. (2002). Chapter 33, *Statutes of 2002*. Sacramento CA: California State Printing Office.

Debates and Proceedings of the Constitutional Convention of the State of California, Vol. I & II. (1880). Sacramento, CA: State Printing Office.

Eastin, D. (1996, June 5). [Correspondence from the California State Superintendent of Instruction to Governor Gray Davis].

EdSource. (1999). Collective bargaining: Explaining California's system. In *Current policy readings: K–12 school reform in California*. Palo Alto, CA: Author.

Fuller, L. (1964). *The morality of law*. New Haven, CT: Yale University Press.

Goss v. Lopez, 419 U.S. 565 (1975).

Grissmer, D., & Flannagan, A. (1998). *Exploring rapid achievement gains in North Carolina and Texas* (Lessons from the States. National Education Goals Panel). Retrieved October 23, 2002, from http://www.negp.gov/reports/grissmer.pdf

Heise, M. (1995). State constitutions, school finance litigation, and the "third wave": From equity to adequacy. *Temple Law Review, 68,* 1151.

Heubert, J. (Ed.). (1999). *Law and school reform: Six strategies for promoting educational equity*. New Haven, CT: Yale University Press.

Kagan, R. (1986). Regulating schools and regulating business. In D. Kirp & D. Jensen (Eds.), *School days, rule days* (pp. 64–90). Philadelphia: Falmer.

Kagan, R. (2001). *Adversarial legalism: The American way of law.* Cambridge, MA: Harvard University Press.
Kirp, D. (1986). Introduction: The fourth R. In D. Kirp & D. Jensen (Eds.), *School days, rule days* (pp. 1–14). Philadelphia: Falmer.
Kirp, D., & Jensen, D. (Eds.). (1986). *School days, rule days.* Philadelphia: Falmer.
Lau v. Nichols, 414 U.S. 563 (1974).
Legislative Analyst. (1984). *Budget analysis 1984–85: Report of the Legislative Analyst.* Sacramento, CA: Office of the Legislative Analyst.
Legislative Analyst. (1999). *K–12 master plan: Starting the process.* Retrieved September 19, 2002, from www.lao.ca.gov/1999_reports/0599_K–12_master_plan.htm
Mills v. Board of Education, 348 F. Supp. 866 (D.D.C. 1972).
Minorini, P., & Sugarman, S. (1999) Education adequacy and the courts: The promise and problems of moving to a new paradigm. In H. Ladd, R. Chalk, & J. Hansen (Eds.), *Equity and adequacy in education finance* (pp. 175–208). Washington, DC: National Academy Press.
No Child Left Behind Act of 2001, Pub. L. No. 107–110, 115 Stat. 1425 (2002).
PARC v. Commonwealth, 334 F. Supp 1257 (1971).
Policy Analysis for California Education. (1995). *Conditions of education in California, 1994–95.* Berkeley, CA: University of California, Graduate School of Education.
Serrano v. Priest, 5 Cal. 3d. 584, 96 Cal Rptr. 601, 487 P. 2d. 1241 (1971). Serrano II 18 Cal. 3d. 728, 135 Cal. Rptr. 345, 557 P. 2d. 929 (1976).
Tiebout, C. M. (1956). A pure theory of local expenditures. *Journal of Political Economy, 64*(5), 416–424.
Timar, T. (1994). Federal education policy and practice: Building organizational capacity through Chapter 1. *Education Evaluation and Policy Analysis, 15,* 51–66.
Timar, T. (2004). *Reform of categorical funding in education in california: Analysis and recommendations.* Berkeley: University of California Press, Policy Analysis for California Education.
Timar, T., Kirst, M., & Kirp, K. (1995). *The role of state agencies in mathematics reform in education.* San Francisco: Far West Laboratory.
Tinker v. Des Moines Independent Community School District, 393 U.S. 503 (1969).
Verstegen, D., & Knoeppel, R. (1998). Equal education under the law: School finance reform and the courts. *The Journal of Law and Politics, 14*(3), 559–589.
Williams v. State of California. (2000a). Superior Court of the State of California, County of San Francisco.
Williams v. State of California. (2000b, November 14). Order on State Demurrer. Superior Court of the State of California, County of San Francisco.
Williams v. State of California. (2003). Plaintiffs' Liability Disclosure Statement, Superior Court of the State of California, County of San Francisco, pp. 324–361.
Yudof, M., Kirp, D., Levin, B., & Moran, R. (2002). *Education policy and law* (4th ed.). Belmont, CA: West-Thompson Learning.

For Product Safety Concerns and Information please contact our EU
representative GPSR@taylorandfrancis.com
Taylor & Francis Verlag GmbH, Kaufingerstraße 24, 80331 München, Germany

www.ingramcontent.com/pod-product-compliance
Lightning Source LLC
Chambersburg PA
CBHW061842300426
44115CB00013B/2478